Bolton Wanderers

One Hundred Years at Burnden Park

Bolton Wanderers

One Hundred Years at Burnden Park

Simon Marland

Breedon Books
Publishing Company
Derby

First published in Great Britain by
The Breedon Books Publishing Company Limited
44 Friar Gate, Derby, DE1 1DA.
1995

Acknowledgements
The author would like to thank the following for their help in
producing this book: the *Bolton Evening News*, Bolton Central Library,
with thanks to individuals Bert Gregory, Glyn Mather, Gordon
Sharrock, and finally to my family whose patience and
understanding in the face of this obsession remains unfailing.

ISBN 1 85983 018 8

Printed and bound by Butler & Tanner, Frome, Somerset.

Contents

Introduction

BURNDEN Park, the home of the Bolton Wanderers, is 100 years old in August 1995. This book is a celebration of those years, covering some of the games and the players who have played a part in the ground's history.

As a small boy, I can still recall the feeling of excitement on approaching the ground for the first time with my father in May 1967. Rushing through the turnstiles at the Embankment to leap up the steps to get a first view of the pitch and the stands that spread out before my eyes.

It was Burnden's final League game of that season and the Wanderers made it a memorable 'debut' for me by defeating Millwall 5-0. From then on I was hooked. For the rest of that summer I was Francis Lee or Brian Bromley, smashing the ball against the garden shed, much to the annoyance of all the neighbours.

From then on it was Burnden every Saturday, alternating between different areas of the ground, watching the reserves when the first team were away until I somehow talked my father into travelling to away games.

The late 1960s and early 1970s were, in retrospect, depressing times at Burnden which culminated in relegation to Division Three for the first time. I remained a super optimist, standing on the Lever End with friends who, at the half-time interval, would re-enact the first half by playing with a plastic cup in the refreshment area. For all of us, this was to be the nearest we would get to playing on Burnden.

The author's first view of Burnden Park in May 1967, a view that can no longer be enjoyed due to the building of the Normid superstore.

In 1973, the tide turned and Burnden once again saw a successful Wanderers team. And for the first time in my life it became a joy to go to school on a Monday morning!

In a throwback to the pre-floodlight days, I had the experience of having to 'bunk' off school to get to midweek afternoon games at Burnden during the power workers' and miners' strikes. A performance of Oscar winning proportions, feigning illness in the morning, would be replaced by a miraculous 'recovery' a couple of hours before kick-off. The ploy didn't convince my teacher and on each occasion I was 'rewarded' with detention which I figured was a fair swop.

An invite to Burnden on the pretext of seeing Frank Worthington's legs was accepted by a girlfriend, who later became my wife when she found my legs were just as nice, even if they weren't as skilful with a football.

These sort of stories are by no means unique. There are many people who have passed through Burnden Park, who could relate specific periods of their life to their visit and to the game taking place.

I cannot explain this mania. I can only fuel it with this book and the fact that those responsible for building Burnden Park would be satisfied that it was still better used than many other places of local entertainment 100 years on.

Simon Marland
Bolton
May 1995

Goodbye Pikes Lane

THE old ground at Pikes Lane had been home to Bolton Wanderers since 1881 and had seen the club rise to become a much-respected founder member of the Football League.

Moves were made to relocate during 1893 when, in the space of five years, the rent had risen from £35 to £175 per annum. The largest attendance on the ground had been for the FA Cup fourth-round replay against Notts County in February 1884 when 18,000 saw County win 2-1. Many, though, had seen the game from outside the grounds boundaries. A local farmer had attempted to sue the Wanderers for damage to his fields by trespassers, but his case fell apart when it was revealed he had collected cash from those wanting to see the game but unable to do so by legitimate means, so he had allowed them to stand in his adjacent field.

As football began to get more popular so the facility at Pikes Lane began to show that it was not capable of future demands. All around the Pikes Lane area property had been springing up and the club's insecurity in holding tenure for the ground was also put in question.

In August 1893 the club's followers were informed that the secretary, Mr J.J.Bentley, had made an offer to the Gas Committee for land at Burnden which had been secured some years previous by the Corporation for extending the gas works. This land was now no longer required for that purpose and was offered to Bolton Wanderers on a 14-year lease for a rent of £150 per annum.

In July 1894, four months after the club had played in its first FA Cup Final, a deputation met the Gas Committee. Messrs J.Magee (local brewer and later to be the club's president), J.J.Bentley (secretary), T.H.Gregson (treasurer) and R.W.Kenyon (official), thrashed out an agreement to take on the land at Burnden for the sum of £130 per annum for 14 years.

The five-acre site, which had previously been used as a tip, needed not only to be built, but rights of way had to be negotiated with the Burnden Tar Distillery Co and the Burnden

This page and overleaf: Scenes at Pikes Lane during the Wanderers' latter days there.

Bleach works. It was agreed that two roads, over which the companies had right of way, would be closed and the Bolton Corporation would substitute these with a new road leading down to the valley from the main Manchester Road.

On 26 October 1894, a general meeting of the club was called with the object of raising funds. It was decided at this meeting to turn the club into a limited liability company, and issue 4,000 shares at £1 each, the title of the new company being The Bolton Wanderers Football and Athletic Company Limited. The Athletic part of the name was derived from the fact that it was decided that the new ground should have, in addition to a football pitch, a cycling and running track.

The new company was incorporated on 15 January 1895 under company registration number 43026. Mr J.W. Makant was elected president and chairman, the other directors being, Mr J.J.Bentley, Mr F.W.Kenyon, Mr J.Magee, Mr T.H.Gregson, Mr J.T.Atkinson, Mr R.Isherwood and Mr R.H.Jackson. Mr A.H.Downs, who had been Bentley's assistant, was elected first secretary.

Only 1,500 of the shares were taken up at the initial meeting but these were later snapped up when subscribers of £25 were awarded a deal which would entitle the holder to two stand seats in perpetuity.

A grounds committee supervised the work on the new ground which was put in the hands of J.O.McQuone from Scarborough. His contractors would transform one of the most desolate parts of Bolton into one fit to host any sporting event.

The whole image of Burnden, which had changed several times in the previous century, was to be more charming to the eye. In 1800 the area had several small bleaching works but was considered to be 'out of town'. In 1838, the Bolton-Manchester railway line was constructed which ran adjacent to the area. Ten years later a branch line to Bury cut across the main road. The discovery of coal in the area brought about more change with the Great Lever Colliery being situated on Raikes Lane and the Rose Hill Colliery being on where the coach park is now at Burnden Park.

In 1870, cottages fronted the entire

length of Manchester Road, whilst a chemical works occupied the site of where the playing pitch was to be constructed.

Within a few months during 1895 the enclosure was constructed. An enormous amount of tipping was required to level the area and turf was laid on a layer of cinders between 12 and 18 inches deep. The laid portion of turf for the pitch measured 118 yards by 80 yards which compared to 112 yards by 74 yards for the start of the 1884-95 season.

Strong barriers outside the cycle track were constructed, the track measuring 18 inches from the inside and one lap was the equivalent of a quarter of a mile. The width of the track was 22 feet, and 28 feet on the bends which were banked up some six feet. It was of a similar style to one that had been laid for the King of Italy.

The grandstand on the Darcy Lever side of the ground was 80 yards long and had ten rows of seats capable of holding 1,600 spectators, the central portion being reserved for 400 persons. This had been erected by Messrs.

Cooper & Son of Bolton. The shelter below the seating area had a facility for 3,000 to stand up whilst two dressing-rooms were constructed, each 22 feet long, the referee having a retiring box.

The Manchester Road side ran for 120 yards and was uncovered with a facility for 5,000 to stand up with an admission price of 9d (4p) in this area. It was hoped that, given time, the club could eventually put a cover over that side of the ground. The south side of Burnden Park, (now the Great Lever End), was a cramped part of the enclosure capable of holding 3,000 spectators. On the North side, the extensive Railway Embankment had to be terraced but was capable of holding around 8,000 standing spectators.

Ten turnstiles were constructed in time for the opening of the ground, the nearest entrance to the main road being by the house that was taken over from the Corporation and was to be used for the groundsman's residence and as the secretary's office. This house was to remain as a landmark until its demolition in 1946.

Pikes Lane was last used for League

Bolton Wanderers in 1883 with the Bolton Charity Cup. Back row (left to right): Kennedy, Dobson, Bromley, McKernan, Steel, J.Parkinson (umpire). Front row: Howarth, Fallon, Struthers, Gleave, Davenport, Scholes.

football on 13 April 1895 when the Wanderers defeated West Bromwich Albion 5-0. A crowd of 10,000 saw Bolton thrash the FA Cup Finalists who were reduced to ten men late in the game with the sending off of their goalkeeper Reader for a 'kneeing offence'. Peter Turnbull grabbed a hat-trick with the other goals coming from Archie Freebairn and Willie Joyce.

Indeed, Pikes Lane was a happy place in the final months of the 1894-95 season. After struggling for the first few months, the Wanderers' last defeat on the ground came at the hands of Small Heath on 24 November 1894, by 2-1. A run of eight League games saw seven victories and one draw with a goal difference of 34 for and nine against.

Away form had cost the club the chance of any major silverware but the Manchester Cup was secured to at least leave Pikes Lane on something of a high note.

The Opening of Burnden Park

BOLTON Wanderers' new ground had a fitting send off at its opening on Saturday, 17 August 1895, and on the following Bank Holiday Monday, the ninth annual sports meeting organised by the club attracted perhaps the largest crowd ever known to attend an athletic meeting in Lancashire.

The new track was rewarded with a splendid class entry such as had never been seen in Bolton previously and, together with the favourable weather on both days, the public opening of the new enclosure was a magnificent success.

On the Saturday, a crowd of almost 20,000 paid receipts of £453 to witness the proceedings, whilst on the Monday there were 15,000 in attendance with £350 being taken. Indeed, the incomplete turnstiles struggled to cope with the crowds who were eager to view not only the proceedings but also the new surroundings.

The ground presented a fine appearance, the vast holiday throng packing the stands and almost covering the side of the railway embankment which afforded a grand view. The terracing on the Embankment Side had not been completed but accommodation in that part of the ground would be greatly extended after the work.

The utmost good humour prevailed

and the crowd were unstinting in their praise for the visiting athletes who seemed well pleased with their reception and the magnificent crowd. Some splendid sport was furnished, especially in the cycle races, the excitement in the final being at fever pitch. In all there were prizes to the value of £230 up for grabs.

The arrangements went like clockwork with the events setting off promptly and the meeting never being allowed to lag behind in time. The principal officials were: handicapper and timekeeper: J.H.Hardwick and J.Gorton; starter: C.C.Harvey; judges: E.A.Davies, E.J.Droongeole, F.T.Norris, T.E.Lee and J.Lewis. The secretary was none other than the Wanderers' club secretary A.H.Downs; the clerk of the course was J.E.Mangnall (who later managed Manchester United) and the gala superintendent was John Atkinson.

The crowd appeared to be well pleased with the surroundings which were much more comfortable than those afforded at the old Pikes Lane ground. The racing men on the whole admired the track, although a few were of the opinion that the corner leading into the home straight could have been wider. The only accident that occurred there during the meeting was when cyclists Summergill and Glazebrook got too far up the track and collided with the rails in making an attempt to get around after being boxed in by other riders.

Mr McQuone, the contractor who had been responsible for building the enclosure, was heartily congratulated for the way he had prepared the track. All the racing men agreed as to the speed properties of the surface which the times of the races showed. The cinder running track gave a little under the feet but this was to be remedied in time for the next meeting.

The final of the cycle one-mile handicap was won by Owen in a time of two minutes 30 seconds, whilst in the five-mile handicap it was an incredible sight to see no less than 31 riders all jostling for position. The 100 yards sprint was won by J.H.Bradley in a time of 10.25 seconds.

The gala programme consisted of a paddock troupe of lady cyclists, sisters St Lava wire performers, Pannell's performing dogs, Comies stilt walker and a dive by Professor J.Bracken, enveloped in a sack, from a trapeze suspended 100 feet from the ground into an eight-foot tank containing only five feet of water. The Halliwell Brass Band performed whilst all this was going on.

Bolton Harriers held their sixth annual sports event at Burnden on 31 August with 5,000 spectators in attendance. The price of admission was sixpence and a shilling with the stands being extra.

Bolton Wanderers had finally got to use the ground on Tuesday, 27 August when a public practice match took place. The event was repeated two days later with about an hour's play being indulged in on both evenings. Football had finally arrived at Burnden Park!

The folk festival spirit of the Wanderers annual athletic meetings, which began in 1887, could be carried over to the new ground at Burnden, but irrelevant matches such as the Wanderers taking on The Aladdin Pantomime Co had to cease to put the club on a more professional footing. This was something of a difficult decision as the game against the Pantomime Co in February 1892, which was in aid of the starving nail makers of Bromsgrove, produced not only 30 goals, but record receipts for a midweek game at Pikes Lane at the time of £76 6s 2d (£76.31p). The League and Cup competitions were now too inflexible to allow such diversions.

Burnden Park officially opened for football on Wednesday, 11 September 1895 when Preston North End were the visitors for a benefit game for Di Jones. The Lillywhites won the game 1-0. Martin scoring the first League goal on the ground for Bolton at the Embankment End.

The Grand Opening

11 September 1895
BOLTON WANDERERS 0 PRESTON NORTH END 1

The opening match on the new ground at Burnden took place for the benefit of Di Jones, the Wanderers captain and Welsh international full-back who had served the club for seven years.

The Trotters faced a strong wind in the first half but, attacking sharply, they found Jim Trainer, the Welsh international and former Bolton goalkeeper, in fine form for North End. Play was rather tame but Blythe for the visitors and Martin for the home side made several good runs. Trainer brought off a grand save from Joyce whilst David Smith shot against the bar for North End, the interval arriving with no score.

Upon resuming Brown got away and troubled Trainer, but North End retaliated, taking a couple of corners that were cleared without difficulty. As darkness began to fall in the final minutes, North End scored what was to be the first goal on the ground, David Smith getting clear to force the ball past Sutcliffe.

Neither side exerted themselves to any extent, both having important League fixtures the following Saturday. The benefit however proved to be a success for a player who was a magnificent servant to the club.

Bolton Wanderers: Sutcliffe; Hamilton, Jones, Paton, McGeachan, Freebairn, Martin, Brown, Joyce, Wright, Cassidy.
Preston North End: Trainer; Tait, Holmes, Sharp, Sanders, Greer, Henderson, Eccleston, D.Smith, T.Smith, Blythe.

Attendance: 3,000
Referee: J.Lewis (Blackburn)

League Football Comes to Burnden Park

14 September 1895
BOLTON WANDERERS 3 EVERTON 1

It was perhaps fitting that Everton should be the first League visitors to Burnden Park as the Wanderers had been the first side to visit the Goodison enclosure for a First Division fixture in September 1892.

Spectators started to roll up at two o'clock, attracted by an hour's cycle scratch race in which most of the local cracks were riding. By three o'clock, an hour before the kick-off, there were close upon 10,000 spectators in the ground, the chances of the teams being freely discussed.

Everton had triumphed in the previous five League games between the clubs along with a Lancashire Cup Final victory the season before last. Special trains from Liverpool, Manchester and Bury brought a large contingent of spectators for what was an ideal football day in weather terms.

The Wanderers were led on to the field by Welshman David Jones and were accorded a splendid reception, Everton being warmly received a few seconds later.

League football at Burnden Park commenced punctually and was set in motion by the home centre-forward William Joyce, the Wanderers kicking towards the railway end of the ground.

Everton were soon reduced to ten men when their centre-half, Holt, collided with Jocky Wright, his cheekbone being so badly cut that he

Opposite page: Welsh international Jimmy Trainer, Bolton's former goalkeeper who played against the Trotters in the first official game at Burnden Park.

had to be carried off and medically attended to. After this stoppage of three minutes, the Wanderers attacked, Wright swinging over a cross that found Jim Martin who rushed the ball past the oncoming goalkeeper 25 minutes after the kick-off.

Jim Cassidy then struck the crossbar for the Trotters, but he was swift enough to follow up and from the ensuing scrimmage made it 2-0. Despite the fact that Everton had only ten men, they continued to have their share of the game and the home defence had to be wary. Seconds from half-time, the visitors made a breakthrough when, from Sutcliffe's long clearance, McInnes secured and sent in a fine long shot which went through into the corner of the goal.

The second half saw the referee's whistle become very prominent whilst Everton were strengthened by the return of Holt. Cassidy again struck the Everton bar but the points were made safe for Bolton when Joyce headed home Wright's corner.

The result ended Everton's unbeaten three-match run at the start of the season, the crowd paying receipts of £372 to witness Bolton's first Burnden success.

Bolton Wanderers: Sutcliffe; Somerville, Jones, Paton, McGeachan, Freebairn, Martin, Brown, Joyce, Wright, Cassidy.
Everton: Hillman; Kelso, Adams, Boyle, Holt, Stewart, McInnes, Bell, Flewitt, Chadwick, Milward.

Attendance: 15,000
Referee: Mr Barker

The Tide Turns
12 March 1898
BOLTON WANDERERS 2 WOLVERHAMPTON WANDERERS 1

The tide of disaster that had swept the Trotters into such a deplorable League position made its effect felt on the attendance at Burnden Park for this First Division game.

Without a League win since November, beaten by a Southern League side in the FA Cup, a Second Division club in the Lancashire Cup and a Lancashire League side in the Manchester Cup, Bolton needed a desperate remedy to change matters.

With only two exceptions, Bolton fielded what was their second team and the small crowd accorded them a hearty reception. Indeed, it would have been a full reserve line up but for an injury to Dan Nichol and a clerical oversight, with regards to Harry Chorlton, who had not been registered with the League, although having played for the reserves all season.

Bolton were guilty during the first half of too much short passing and it was the visitors who held the initiative at the interval. Their goal came from a centre by Tonks which found Beats and his shot caught the inside of the post before entering the goal.

The game began to degenerate into a scramble in which two or three of the Trotters tried to do by force what they could not manage by reality.

Ten minutes from time Bolton finally got through to equalise. It came from a Thompson centre that eluded everyone and fell for Jim Cassidy to roll over the line.

After a rush by Wolves, Gregory carried the ball along the left to centre beautifully for Cassidy to gather the ball and beat Baddeley for a second time with a grand shot.

The Wolves defence now collapsed and both Brown and Freebairn went close to increasing Bolton's advantage.

Bolton Wanderers: Lee; Somerville, Davies, Fitchett, Brown, Freebairn, Thompson, Gilligan, T.Miller, Cassidy, Gregory.

Wolverhampton Wanderers: Baddeley; Eccles, Blackett, Griffiths, Owen, Fleming, Tonks, Wood, Beats, Smith, Millar.

Attendance: 4,000
Referee: J.Miller

Down for the First Time
17 April 1899
BOLTON WANDERERS 0 ASTON VILLA 0

The visit of Aston Villa to Burnden Park for the Trotters' last First Division match for an indefinite period drew a very 'raw' attendance of spectators. The weather being of a far different description than that on the New Year's Day game when Villa were last at Bolton and the game was abandoned with the Wanderers leading by 1-0 just after half-time.

There was a melancholy interest in the 5.20pm kick-off on a Monday afternoon, the visitors being anxious to secure the points by reason for the close struggle in which they were engaged with Liverpool for the championship of the League. For the Wanderers it was to be a case of departing from the First Division gracefully and not having the wooden spoon.

The game opened quietly, Freebairn showed that he was in fine form by denying the Villa forwards, but they came again and with a splendid long shot Wheldon hit the post, Athersmith failing to convert the rebound.

As the game progressed Wheldon and Smith were busy on the left wing but Fitchett tackled them in rare style and the Wanderers held their own. Somerville, however, missed a challenge on Wheldon and it looked all up a Villa goal but an extraordinary effort by Sutcliffe, who came out and threw himself at Wheldon's feet, saved a goal.

The cheering was quite hearty at this and the Wanderers, thankful for their escape, took up the running, Jack delivering a low cross that no one could convert.

John Sutcliffe – Wanderers' English international goalkeeper who kept a clean sheet in his side's goalless draw against Villa.

Villa increased the pace of the game after half-time, Sutcliffe knocking out a number of shots. During the last ten minutes Bolton put marvellous vigour into their play. They came out with considerable credit and might have won during their closing attacks which saw Villa's defence stretched.

Bolton Wanderers: Sutcliffe; Somerville, R.Davies, Fitchett, Hynds, Freebairn, Morgan, Gilligan, McAteer, Barlow, Jack.

Aston Villa: George; Spencer, Evans, Bowman, Cowan, Crabtree, Athersmith, Davey, Garraty, Wheldon, Smith.

Attendance: 5,000

Referee: Mr Barker

Burnden Tastes Second Division Football

9 September 1899
BOLTON WANDERERS 2 NEWTON HEATH 1

An excellent opportunity was afforded of measuring the extent of both teams when the Trotters opened their first-ever Second Division home programme with a visit from Newton Heath.

The Trotters had entered upon the season's work in a highly satisfactory manner, following up their opening day victory at Loughborough Town with a creditable friendly draw at Burnley in midweek and they felt confident after the result.

Rain threatened as Bolton kicked towards the Town End and immediately made tracks for the visitors' goal. Picken was illegally brought down but the free-kick came to nothing, the Heathens then having an attack by Bryant and Jackson repelled.

Freebairn won the ball from Bryant with a stiff challenge and from a pass by Bell, Jack was afforded a good opening only to be robbed by Stafford. The Boltonians strode out to score and Barlow was brought down in a favourable position but the referee returned immediately to play and some unpleasantness was diffused.

Bolton came to the end of the first half with only ten men, Lockhart having been injured. Two quick corners saw the home side pressure the Manchester men, Laurie Bell finding the net from the latter.

The Trotters increased their lead early in the second half, Bell being a little surprised to see his long shot fly past Barrett and end up in the net.

Newton Heath came back into the game in the latter stages, Ambler opening their account. Inspired by this success, Heath attacked the Bolton goal in an effort to earn a point but Sutcliffe was equal to all that they could throw at him.

The Wanderers had made the ideal start in their attempt to make their absence from the First Division as short as possible.

Bolton Wanderers: Sutcliffe; Halley, Lockhart, Brown, McAteer, Freebairn, Morgan, Picken, Bell, Barlow, Jack.
Newton Heath: Barrett; Stafford, Erentz, Morgan, Griffiths, Cartwright, Bryant, Jackson, Lee, Gaffey, Ambler.

Attendance: 6,000
Referee: Mr Ackton (Bury)

Laurie Bell, who hit both Bolton goals that defeated Newton Heath in the first-ever Second Division game on Burnden. Bell went on to become Wanderers' leading scorer that season with 23 goals.

Burnden ...International Class

11 November 1899
ENGLISH LEAGUE 3 IRISH LEAGUE 1

Unfortunately for everyone, the poor state of the weather, ominously gloomy with a strong blustery wind, assisted greatly to have a disastrous effect upon the attendance for this Inter-League challenge match.

The match had excited great interest with Lancashire being well represented in the English team. An additional attraction to Boltonians was the presence of John Fitchett, the Wanderers right half-back, whose selection had given great satisfaction locally.

Fitchett had joined the Wanderers from West Manchester and made his League debut on his 17th birthday against Sunderland in February 1898.

Through their previous performances, the Irish League team had failed to prove themselves, but there was a great desire to take advantage of the opportunity afforded by the appointment of Burnden Park for a match of such importance.

It was the first occasion that Burnden had been so favoured and when the Irishmen appeared, their apparel allowing of no mistake to their identity, they sought shelter from the boisterous elements in the dressing-room.

At 3pm the Irishmen kicked off with the advantage of the strong wind.

The English League opened the scoring after 14 minutes, Johnson of Stoke speeding away on the right in fine style before dropping an inch-perfect cross for Settle, the Evertonian scoring with ridiculous ease.

Two minutes from the interval Aston Villa back, Spencer, headed through his own goal when under pressure from the Irish League centre McAuley.

Eight minutes after the restart Bloomer put England back in front with a characteristic shot and late in the game he made it safe when he beat Benton with a goal from close range.

English League: Birchenough (Burslem Port Vale); Spencer (Aston Villa), Williams (West Bromwich Albion), Fitchett (Bolton Wanderers), Leeming (Bury), Needham (Sheffield United), Johnson (Stoke), Bloomer (Derby County), Beats (Wolves), Settle (Everton), Hurst (Blackburn Rovers).

Irish League: Benton (Glentoran); Cochrane (Distillery), Leeman (Distillery), Nichol (Belfast Celtic), Matthews (Distillery), McMaster (Glentoran), Darling (Linfield), Smyth (Distillery), McAuley (Belfast Celtic), Johnson (Glentoran), McAllen (Linfield).

Attendance: 5,372
Referee: Jas McPherson (Scottish League)

Promotion Hopes Strengthened
13 January 1900
BOLTON WANDERERS 1 SHEFFIELD WEDNESDAY 0

Though the announcement that this game was billed as the decider for the championship of the Second Division, it required no deep study of the present state of affairs to discover the great importance of the match to both sides.

The Wanderers, Wednesday and Leicester Fosse had broken clear at the top, separated by only two points, each club having lost only one game. In Bolton's case this game was opportunity for revenge having lost by 2-1 at Owlerton the previous September.

Bolton had to make alterations to the team selected, Archie Freebairn being unfit, Tom McAteer moving to centre-half and 'Sparrow' Brown being handed the captain's role.

Former Wanderer Jocky Wright,

Wednesday's leading scorer, roused the fire of the crowd early on with a deliberate foul on McAteer.

A sparkling run by Picken and Jack was frustrated by Ferrier but the attack was renewed and Hanson headed just over for Bolton.

The game was being fiercely contested with the Wanderers having the slight edge. Jack flew down the wing in delightful style and finished up with an effort that Wednesday goalkeeper Massey could only fist down. Morgan appeared to have capitalised on the mistake but placed his shot in front of an open goal, wide of the target.

Bolton went ahead in the 65th minute, Bell fastening on to a loose ball and sending it goalwards, Jack beating

Massey to it and slipping it into the empty net.

Stimulated by this success the Wanderers made further attempts and the game was a well-fought affair to the finish.

On the same day, Leicester Fosse lost at Burton Swifts and both Bolton and Sheffield began to get clear in the promotion race, the Yorkshire club eventually winning the race for the championship, the Wanderers being runners-up.

Bolton Wanderers: Sutcliffe; Somerville, Halley, Fitchett, McAteer, R.N.Brown, Morgan, Hanson, Bell, Picken, Jack.
Sheffield Wednesday: Massey; Layton, Langley, Ferrier, Crawshaw, Ruddlesden, Brash, Price, Miller, Wright, Spiksley.
Attendance: 12,325
Referee: A.Kingscott (Derby)

Burnden's First FA Cup Shock
23 February 1901
BOLTON WANDERERS 0 READING 1

The good fortune that the Trotters experienced in being drawn at home in the first round of the FA Cup, when they defeated Derby County, was again enjoyed at the second stage of the competition.

They had the advantage of being the only First Division side still left in the competition to have been drawn at home and their task was considered to be one of the easiest against the southern outfit.

The Biscuitmen were expecting at least a draw, the teams prior to this game, having been entire strangers.

The Trotters had not been in any special training for the tie whilst, Reading had been at Nettlebed, one of the highest points in the South of England, and they had spent the night at The Swan Hotel.

Having lost the toss, Reading started towards the Town End and immediately made tracks for the Wanderers' goal, Pegg missing a splendid opportunity from a pass by Barnes.

Tracey had an electrifying shot which hit the side netting for Bolton but in general the visitors' defence was rarely troubled. This pattern continued into the second half, Tracey forcing a corner off Clinch, following which Picken made a glorious attempt but Cotton saved well.

Six minutes after the restart Evans forced a corner for the visitors which resulted in Sharp shooting past Sutcliffe to put the underdogs ahead.

Reading went close to increasing their lead before Bolton maintained a terrific assault on their goal in an attempt to equalise.

Goalkeeper Cotton and his defenders did extremely well to keep their house in order and, as the game wore on, the Wanderers did little to suggest that they would force a replay.

Burnden Park had seen its first FA Cup shock.

Bolton Wanderers: Sutcliffe; Brown, Woolfall, Lowe, McAteer, Freebairn, Smith, Bell, McKie, Picken, Tracey.
Reading: Cotton; J.Sharp, Clinch, Bull, Mainman, Watts Evans, Logan, A.Pegg, Sharp, Barnes.

Attendance: 11,592
Referee: A.J.Barker (Hanley)

Pie Saturday for the FA Cup Final Replay

27 April 1901
TOTTENHAM HOTSPUR 3 SHEFFIELD UNITED 1

What town throughout the length, and breadth of the country did not envy Bolton of the honour that fell to her in the shape of hosting the greatest match of the English football season with this FA Cup Final?

The thriving Lancashire town rose to the honour of the occasion since the decision had been made to host the game and the environs had become a fever of excitement.

When it was considered that it had been seven years since a similar event had taken place in the Provinces, the intense interest which was centred in the game could be understood.

Only three times had the Final been played outside London, in 1886 when Blackburn won the trophy at Derby in a replayed game, in 1893 when Wolves triumphed at Fallowfield and in 1894 when Bolton themselves lost to Notts County at Goodison.

Despite the enthusiasm of the locals there were many rumours of protest against the unsuitability of the ground, the insufficient accommodation and the poor means of outlet for the expected immense crowd and this possibility gave rise for many non-attenders.

The Wanderers themselves went to great lengths to increase accommodation, special seats being erected on the cycle track, the immense Embankment terraced and it was reckoned 50,000 could be accommodated with ease.

It was of great disappointment that the railway companies declined to provide cheap travel facilities and this deterred many Lancashire football supporters from attending.

As it turned out just over 20,000 attended, the occasion becoming known as Pie Saturday on account of the catering miscalculations by the Bolton's bakers. Pies were being given away that evening in the town!

As for the game, Priest gave Sheffield United a first-half advantage, but Tottenham became the first Southern League club to secure the Cup with second-half strikes from Cameron, Smith and Brown.

The trophy was presented to Spurs by the president of the FA, Lord Kinnaird.

Scene from the only FA Cup Final to be held at Burnden. Note the only covered area on the ground was the old Darcy Lever Stand – where the Burnden Stand is now situated.

Tottenham Hotspur: Clawley; Erentz, Tait, Morris, Hughes, Jones, Smith, Cameron, Brown, Copeland, Kirwan.
Sheffield United: Foulke; Boyle, Thickett, Johnson, Morren, Needham, Bennett, Field, Hedley, Priest, Lipsham.

Attendance: 20,740
Referee: A.Kingscott (Derby)

More action with the Sheffield United goalkeeper, Foulke, looking rather menacingly at the grounded Spurs player.

New Year's Day Extravaganza
1 January 1902
BOLTON WANDERERS 3 MANCHESTER CITY 3

Although the Trotters' acquaintance in League football with Manchester City was only of a season's duration, the greatest rivalry existed between the clubs and was clearly demonstrated in this New Year's Day encounter.

After two poor attendances at Burnden for the visit of Stoke and Sunderland, a crowd of almost 20,000 presented a splendid appearance when the teams turned out.

Sutcliffe won the toss for Bolton and they defended the Great Lever End, going ahead before two minutes had elapsed. Bell won possession and combined with Barlow to turn the ball inside for Williams to celebrate his return to the first team with an unstoppable shot.

Both teams were persistent and play fluctuated rapidly from end to end, City's Billy Meredith treating the crowd to a good sample of his abilities, making a brilliant run that was matched only by Sutcliffe's incredible save.

The Wanderers grabbed their second goal in the 27th minute, a corner from Williams finding centre-half Bannister who headed powerfully past Barrett.

Ten minutes from half-time City got back into the game when Hurst's cross found Meredith, who eluded both Ostick and Taylor before shooting home from close quarters.

Laurie Bell scored his seventh goal of the season soon after the restart to increase Bolton's advantage, injured full-back William Brown having a hand in the build-up.

City kept themselves in the game with a goal from Howe, who found the net by virtue of a shot from 25 yards, and late in the proceedings the visitors struck again to earn themselves a point.

Henderson set up the chance by drawing out the Bolton defence before playing through to Ross, who found the net at the second attempt.

Despite the disappointment in losing a point, the match proved to be a springboard for four consecutive League wins, a feat that the Wanderers hadn't performed in the First Division since 1896.

Bolton Wanderers: Sutcliffe; W.Brown, Ostick, Freebairn, Bannister, Taylor, Bell, Picken, McKie, Barlow, Williams.
Manchester City: Barrett; Orr, Slater, Smith, Hynds, Howe, Meredith, Ross, Henderson, H.Jones, Hurst.

Attendance: 19,353
Referee: T.P.Campbell (Blackburn)

Burnden Tastes Victory ...at Last
24 January 1903
BOLTON WANDERERS 2 DERBY COUNTY 0

After Bolton had won their first Division One game of the season at the 23rd attempt the previous Saturday, a 3-1 success at Notts County, there was a more than passing interest in Derby's visit to Burnden.

Bolton fielded the same side that had finally tasted a victory whilst Derby were without Steve Bloomer and they gave a debut to Scottish international Johnny May.

The home goal had two narrow escapes in the opening minutes, debutant May forcing Fred Thompson into good saves.

From their first advantage the Trotters had the ball in the net, Bob Taylor crashing home from a pass by Sam Marsh; the goal however, was rightly disallowed for offside.

Walter White had a grand effort well saved by Fryer in the Derby goal but he couldn't prevent Bolton going ahead after seven minutes play.

Taylor feigned a pass before applying his foot to the ball, stopped and lifted it high into the net from 18 yards out.

Bolton then attacked with greater force than before and continued to monopolise the play. Unfortunately their shooting wasn't compatible with their build up play and, try as they might, Derby could not reverse the tide which flowed against them.

It wasn't until the 65th minute that the home side increased their lead, Marsh winding up a glorious piece of work when he wriggled his way past both backs and with one of his terrific shots gave Fryer no chance.

Thompson saw very little of the ball until the final ten minutes but by then the Wanderers had fallen away and were confining themselves to defence.

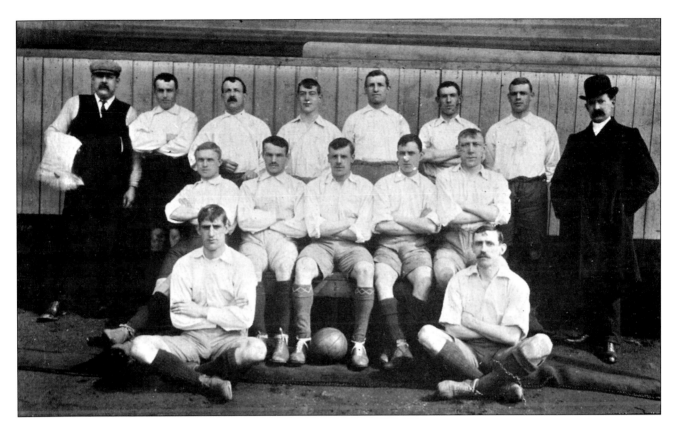

At the 11th attempt the Wanderers had finally registered a home win for the patrons of Burnden to savour. Talk was now of avoiding relegation – an impossible task – but a further six wins before the season's end regained some lost pride.

Bolton Wanderers: Thompson; Holliday, Struthers, Freebairn, Greenhalgh, Boyd, Hanson, White, Marsh, McKay, Taylor.
Derby County: Fryer; Methven, Morris, Warren, Goodall, Leckie, May, Warrington, Yorke, Richards, Davis.
Attendance: 10,000
Referee: A.J.Barker (Hanley)

Bolton Wanderers in 1904. Back row (left to right): J.Lewis (trainer), R.Brown, J.Freebairn, S.Greenhalgh, D.Davies, J.Boyd, R.Struthers, J.J.Bentley. Front row: D.Stokes, S.Marsh, W.Yenson, W.White, R.Taylor. On ground: R.Clifford, J.Wright.

Hat-tricks for Marsh and White
19 November 1904
BOLTON WANDERERS 7 BURTON UNITED 1

After a dozen games the Second Division promotion race appeared to be a three-horse race between the Wanderers. Liverpool and Manchester United.

Burnden Park had never been a happy hunting ground for Burton United and they had lost their last two League games heavily. They had nothing but defeat staring them in the face as the Wanderers appeared before their own patrons for the third consecutive week, looking to keep up a 100 per cent home record.

In the opening half minute Walter White put a centre into the Burton goalmouth and Sam Marsh was on hand to put Bolton one up when he steered the ball into the gaping goal.

The second goal came in the 20th minute, Burton 'keeper Bromage being unable to hold a shot from Albert Shepherd and Marsh was on him in a twinkling to brush the ball over the line.

On the half-hour White made it three when he swept home a David Stokes cross and the cheers had hardly died down when Shepherd made it four with an oblique shot.

Just before half-time Gould hooked the ball through whilst falling on his

Bolton Wanderers in 1904-05. Back row (left to right): J.Lewis (trainer), J.Freebairn, G.Eccles, R.Clifford, W.Yenson, R.Struthers. Middle row: D.Stokes, A.Shepherd, D.Davies, W.White, R.Taylor. Front row: A.Taylor, S.Marsh, J.Boyd, S.Greenhalgh, T.Wilson. At the end of the season Wanderers were promoted as Second Division runners-up. Walter White hit three of his 24 League goals during 1904-05 against Burton United at Burnden. His striking partner Sam Marsh also notched a hat-trick.

back for Burton. From a Tom Wilson corner, early in the second half, White steered the ball home with full-back Aston evidently under the impression that it would go wide, then Marsh completed his hat-trick when he got the better of both Wildin and Kirkland to bring up the half-dozen.

White completed the rout and his hat-trick, whilst in the final minutes Burton were reduced to ten men when the old Derby custodian, Bromage, was injured in preventing Shepherd from increasing the score.

This was the first occasion that two

Bolton players had notched hat-tricks in the same League game, the club having hit 38 League goals in the first dozen games, more than any other Second Division club.

Bolton Wanderers: Davies; Ostick, Struthers, Clifford, Greenhalgh, Boyd, Stokes, Marsh, Shepherd, White, Wilson.
Burton United: Bromage; Aston, Kirkland, Frost, Mann, Wildin, Beddow, Evans, Hargreaves, Gould, King.

Attendance: 6,000
Referee: A.Hargreaves (Blackpool)

The First of Nine Consecutive Wins
1 January 1906
BOLTON WANDERERS 6 WOOLWICH ARSENAL 1

After a gruelling series of four First Division matches away in a week that hadn't produced a win, the Wanderers were welcomed back to Burnden Park by a magnificent assembly of their own supporters.

Both clubs had been struggling in the lower reaches of the First Division but this game was to set Bolton off on a run of nine consecutive wins that would

give them a top-six spot. It took only four minutes for Bolton to open their account, Walter White screwing a long bouncing shot that the Arsenal 'keeper allowed to bounce past him and just inside the upright.

From a Marshall McEwan corner, four minutes later, Sam Marsh made it 2-0 when he jabbed his right foot at a loose ball to steer it into the corner of

The Manchester Road Stand under construction in 1905. The cycling track was also dismantled at the same time.

The Manchester Road Stand completed – note the bench seats on both the Great Lever and Embankment sides. The ground was also on a level rather being raised as in the present day.

the net. White hit the Wanderers' third goal from a David Stokes corner-kick but Woolwich didn't seem at all dispirited by these startling reverses and the home goal had lucky escapes when Baverstock and Kay had to clear their lines.

Albert Shepherd initiated the Wanderers fourth goal in the 21st minute, setting Stokes away. His cross

The Bolton side that drew 3-3 with Notts County in September 1905. After defeating Arsenal 6-1 on New Year's Day, Bolton also won their next eight games to finish sixth in the First Division.

found Marsh who was on it like a flash with a lightning ground shot.

On the restart, after an unusually long break, Arsenal played with more effect but couldn't prevent Shepherd heading the Trotters' fifth goal from a McEwan corner.

Straight from the kick-off another corner was won and this time Stokes sent the ball over to McEwan who swung it into the net with his right foot to make up the half dozen.

The next attack was made by the visitors who forced a corner on the right. Garbutt dropped the ball in smartly and Satterthwaite headed in with the Wanderers' 'keeper Dai Davies only helping the ball into his own net.

Bolton Wanderers: Davies; Baverstock, Kay, Wolstenholme, Clifford, Boyd, Stokes, Marsh, Shepherd, White, McEwan.
Woolwich Arsenal: Ashcroft; Cross, Sharp, Bigden, Gray, Theobald, Garbutt, Bellamy, Coleman, Satterthwaite, Neave.

Attendance: 21,000
Referee: T.Kirkham (Burslem)

Burnden's First 50,000 Gate

27 February 1907
BOLTON WANDERERS 0 EVERTON 3

Interest in this Cup replay wasn't confined to just Bolton and Liverpool, it was Lancashire derby day with cheap railway bookings bringing in spectators from all over the county.

Over 50,000 had witnessed a goalless draw at Goodison four days earlier between the clubs who were both in the top six of the First Division.

Both sides found it necessary to make alterations from that game. Ex-Glossoponian Billy Cameron replaced the injured Albert Shepherd for Bolton and Wilson appeared at inside-left in place of Rouse for the Cup holders.

Fortunately, for the financial success of the match, the fog which had enveloped the town up until noon rapidly disappeared and the weather turned bright and sunny.

It is safe to say that Burnden, in its near 12 year existence, had never been a venue of such pressure and animation as it was prior to this game. There were over 30,000 inside an hour before the start, staring down on a pitch bare of grass. In quick time the stands were crowded to the door, the old cycle track was really besieged, many workshops having closed at noon and in nearly all cases where employers refused to grant requests for time off, workmen simply took French leave.

And so the first attendance of over 50,000 at Burnden saw the game get under way seven minutes late with the Wanderers kicking towards the Embankment.

A scrimmage in front of goal after 22 minutes ended in a corner-kick that was scrambled home by Taylor to put Everton ahead.

Though the Wanderers played with great energy and enthusiasm, they spent most of the time defending. After Young had been checked close in by Clifford the ball was put back to Abbott who steadied himself and increased Everton's advantage with a splendidly judged long shot from 20 yards.

After the players had left the field for half-time, the encroachment of the crowd seemed likely to cause trouble but the mounted police kept the poachers in check. The second half was only eight minutes old when Young broke off along the centre. Pretty passing between himself and Settle proved too much for Stanley and Baverstock and, though Edmondson ran out and diverted Young's shot, the ball travelled on to Settle who had nothing more to do than scrape it into the net for Everton's third.

The game had now been settled but the Trotters' blue and white umbrellas, rattles, bugles and what not still contributed to the scene.

A grander spring day could not have been desired. Who shared in the remarkable midweek football carnival? Many an employer would perhaps have liked to have known that.

It was suggested that a large number of distant relatives and grandfathers probably died the previous weekend and the interments were supposed to have taken place on match-day, the mourners of course gazing down on a grassless Burnden Park!

Bolton Wanderers: Edmondson; Baverstock, Stanley, Gaskell, Clifford, Boyd, Stokes, Owen, Cameron, White, McEwan.
Everton: Scott; W.Balmer, R.Balmer, Makepeace, Taylor, Abbott, Sharp, Settle, Young, Wilson, Hardman.

Attendance: 54,470
Referee: T.P.Campbell (Blackburn)

Relegation Cliffhanger for the Trotters
25 April 1908
BOLTON WANDERERS 0 NOTTS COUNTY 1

The visit of Notts County to Burnden Park was not only the Wanderers' last First Division game of the season but their last chance of escaping relegation to Division Two.

One point from this game would have been sufficient to make them secure but defeat would leave them at the mercy of Notts, who would then finish one point above them provided they were successful at Chelsea the following Wednesday.

The Wanderers had already won at Notts thanks to a goal from Albert Shepherd and they had also won an English Cup second-round tie after a replay. Indeed it was almost six years since Notts had last taken the points from Bolton and an unchanged side felt confident of the task that lay before

The Bolton side which suffered relegation in 1908. Centre-forward Albert Shepherd, (with the ball at his feet) still managed to strike 25 goals, though.

them. The morning snow had melted, leaving the turf in good condition although a cold wind was blowing in from the Great Lever End.

Shepherd tried an early dash which was cleared by Montgomery and twice Clifford was cheered for breaking up County attacks.

Play was only five minutes old when Gaskell, in trying to hook the ball away, put it to centre and dashing in was Cantrell who hit a fast long shot which beat Davies as he dived full length.

Notts gained confidence from this goal and took the initiative with Matthews having an effort disallowed for offside, Bolton having to defend for all they were worth.

The second half saw a turn around with Bolton going all out for that important equaliser. Penalty appeals were turned down and the County goal had a number of hair's breadth escapes but it was all to no avail.

And so Bolton's last chance of saving themselves had gone. There was still a slender thread of hope that Chelsea would save them and defeat Notts at Stamford Bridge the following midweek, but County saved themselves by taking the points from their visit to London.

Bolton Wanderers: Davies; Slater, Stanley, Gaskell, Clifford, Boyd, Stokes, McClarence, Shepherd, White, McEwan.
Notts County: Iremonger; Morley, Montgomery, Emberton, Clamp, Griffiths, Harper, Matthews, Cantrell, Jones, Dodds.
Attendance: 15,000
Referee: J.T.Ibbotson (Derby)

Champions! Champions!
30 April 1909
BOLTON WANDERERS 1 DERBY COUNTY 0

The last spasm of excitement in a most memorable of seasons gripped the Wanderers and their supporters for a game that, if won, would give them the Second Division championship only a year after the disappointment of relegation.

Public interest in the club's fortunes had risen tremendously during the final month with only one defeat in 11

games. In order to ensure the completion of this Friday fixture, and as a safeguard against interference from defective light, the League Management Committee had ordered a 4.30pm kick-off. The Wanderers made persistent appeals and in response they consented to a half-hour delay in the proceedings.

There was little to choose between the sides in the early stages, the crowd waiting with increasing anxiety for the Wanderers' opening goal.

Bevan was industrious in the centre for Derby and in one incident missed the post by inches. The first half ended with the Derby defence having overshadowed the Bolton attack who were not as dominating as had been anticipated.

The start of the second half was delayed to allow more spectators into the ground and they didn't have to wait long to witness the breakthrough.

Hunter dashed in a vain attempt to rush Atkin off his feet, and, though he did not succeed, the ball fell to Billy Hughes who breasted it down, took deliberate aim and beat Scattergood with a high shot that went into the net near the angle of the woodwork.

After this, the game as a spectacle deteriorated, the importance of the occasion being against good football.

Although the Wanderers appeared anxious, suffering from the intense excitement that was being generated around the ground, they were never in any apparent danger of losing their lead which meant the championship and their return to the First Division along with Spurs was assured.

Bolton Wanderers: Edmondson; Baverstock, Slater, Gaskell, Robinson, Greenhalgh, Stokes, Hogan, Hughes, Owen, Hunter.
Derby County: Scattergood; Atkin, Morris, Barbour, Hall, Bagshaw, Trueman, Garry, Bevan, Barnes, Davies.

Attendance: 30,000
Referee: H.S.Bamlett (Gateshead)

Bolton Wanderers, the Second Division champions in 1908-09 Back row (left to right): A.Gaskell, W.Robinson, H.Baverstock, J.Edmondson, J.Slater, T.Barber. Front row: S.Greenhalgh, J.Hogan, W.Hughes,J. Owen, M.McEwan. On ground: D.Stokes, W.Hunter.

Non-Leaguers End FA Cup Interest

14 January 1911
BOLTON WANDERERS 0 CHESTERFIELD 2

The visit of Chesterfield for this FA Cup first-round tie, recalled the fact that the last time the Wanderers were drawn at home in the first round they beat Woking with ease. Many supporters were strongly optimistic of their ability to deal with an equal force.

The Midland League side had lost their Football League status two years previously and in their four previous visits to Burnden had managed to score only one goal.

There was more than a suspicion of leisurely tactics about the early work of the Wanderers, Ted Vizard losing one grand chance by holding the ball too long.

The ground offered a very treacherous foothold for it was soft on top and frozen underneath, Harold Hilton twice coming to grief in attempting to take up passes.

Chesterfield had a large number of followers and they soon had something to cheer about as Bolton were penned into their own half for some time. After several shots had been charged down Revill finally hit the target with 14 minutes played.

Although Bolton were notoriously bad starters, the Second Division promotion chasers still couldn't make any headway against a determined Chesterfield defence.

A heavy mist descended just before half-time making it difficult to see from one end of the pitch to the other, the visitors being in control of the play.

There was a distinct improvement by the Wanderers in the second half, several successive corners were forced but Chesterfield's goal held firm.

In the 66th minute, Revill, an 18-year-old coal-miner, broke through and his shot beat Edmondson and went into the net off the upright.

The final quarter of an hour was a farce with both fog and semi-darkness causing problems. Captain Sam Greenhalgh, was unwilling, however, to appeal against the light, possibly preferring the thought not to be entertained that he and his men were showing the white feather.

It was an inauspicious start by both Ted Vizard and Joe Smith to the FA Cup competition, both playing in their first tie, but later to become Cup heroes. Bolton were, however, victims of their failure to appreciate the strength of their opponents.

Bolton Wanderers: Edmondson; Stott, Baverstock, Marsh, Greenhalgh, Barber, Stokes, Hilton, Hughes, Smith, Vizard.
Chesterfield: Summers; Cuthbert, Strettle, Thacker, Derby, Munday, Mitlar, Revill, Raybould, Bovill, Stevens.
Attendance: 6,193
Referee: A.H.Oakley (Wolverhampton)

A Quick Return to Division One

26 April 1911
BOLTON WANDERERS 2 CHELSEA 0

A Second Division game of Cup-tie proportions brought Burnden Park's largest attendance since the FA Cup-tie with Everton in 1907.

The race for promotion to the First Division was a three-horse affair between the Wanderers, Chelsea and West Brom, who were all level on 49 points from 36 games.

The attendance was all the more remarkable in view of the many who were lured away to Old Trafford for an exceptional treat in the shape of an English Cup Final. There were, however, hundreds who spared neither expense nor inconvenience with the object of witnessing both games.

As soon as the state of the game would warrant the conclusion that Bradford City would beat Newcastle, hundreds of people made, by every conceivable mode of transport, for the evening kick-off at Burnden Park.

Here they saw a contest which was streets ahead of the Cup Final in the quality of football shown. The decision of the Wanderers management to delay the game long enough to enable mill and other workers to see the start brought forth a tremendous response.

The footwork of Vivian Woodward and the dash and shooting power of Whittingham was a pronounced feature of the game but there was nothing in the Pensioners play to come up to the work of Bolton's tried and trusty left wing of Smith and Vizard.

Six minutes from the start Whiteside dropped in a lovely ball from a free-kick and Hilton, finding himself gloriously placed, forced it straight into the corner of the net.

The second goal, 22 minutes after the interval, followed an admirable centre by Vizard, Hilton again dashing the ball into goal. There was a lively demonstration of satisfaction as the Wanderers made for the dressing-room, several players being carried off by crowds of admirers.

West Bromwich won their final two games to secure the championship and although the Wanderers lost their final game at Birmingham, they accompanied them into Division One as Chelsea lost at Gainsborough Trinity.

Bolton Wanderers: Edmondson; Stott, Baverstock, Marsh, Greenhalgh, E. Whiteside, Stokes, Hilton, Barber, Smith, Vizard.

Chelsea: Molyneux; Cartwright, Cameron, McKenzie, Ormiston, Downing, Brown, Woodward, Whittingham, Freeman, Bridgeman.

Attendance: 38,613
Referee: J.G.A.Sharpe (Lichfield)

Sam Greenhalgh, who captained the Wanderers to promotion back to Division One after a season's absence.

Going for the Bonus
27 April 1912
BOLTON WANDERERS 1 MANCHESTER UNITED 1

The Wanderers last First Division match of 1911-12 was not invested for them with any of the usual end-of-season apathy. Its result meant solid cash to the players, for a win meant a chance of third position, carrying with it a League bonus of £165 and the best finishing position since the opening of Burnden.

For United, the match meant nothing more than the attainment of a position in the table more in keeping with their dignity, but they had for opponents neighbouring rivals, and that made the game interesting.

Wanderers goalkeeper Joe Edmondson led out the Bolton side, this being his benefit from which he would receive £300 from the receipts, and there was another cheer when he won the toss.

The first incident of note was when West placed the ball sweetly for Hamill to run in for a fine opening, but the inside man touched the ball a trifle too far, and out came Edmondson to clear

The Bolton Wanderers players of 1911-12 who were responsible for a creditable fourth place in Division One.

BOLTON WANDERERS Season 1911-12

ECCLES (TRAINER)

BAVERSTOCK   EDMONDSON   STOTT   NEWTON   FEEBURY   TYLDESLEY   SLATER

GREENHALGH   GIMBLETT   MARSH   WHITESIDE (F)   DODDS   BARBER

HILTON   HOGAN   BENTLEY   STOKES   EGERTON

HOBSON   HUNTER   HUGHES   SMITH   VIZARD   PRITCHARD

JONES   COPYRIGHT PHOTOS BY C.E. WILLIS BOLTON   GRIFFITHS

with a long punt. Meredith had several openings for United but the ball was too lively for him.

The Wanderers opened the second half in great style with a goal at the end of four minutes. There was nothing very striking preceding it until Stokes put across a really high centre into the goalmouth at which Joe Smith headed, the ball finding a final resting place in the net for his 22nd League goal of the season.

A moment later the visitors goal was almost captured a second time, for the same player hit the underside of the crossbar.

There was only three minutes left to play when Bolton conceded an equaliser that was to cost them third place in the League and the sum of £55 in bonuses.

Wall fired the ball across to the right and Meredith, taking it on the bounce as it dropped behind Roberts, shot obliquely into the net.

Bolton Wanderers: Edmondson; Stott, Baverstock, Gimblett, Greenhalgh, Barber, Stokes, Hogan, Hughes, Smith, Vizard.
Manchester United: Moger; Linkson, Stacey, Knowles, Roberts, Bell, Meredith, Hamill, West, Nuttall, Wall.

Attendance: 17,935
Referee: S.D.Peers (Liverpool)

Smith Routs United

3 January 1914
BOLTON WANDERERS 6 MANCHESTER UNITED 1

Division One championship chasers Manchester United were handed a lesson by an irresistible Bolton side that completed the double, having won at Old Trafford earlier in the season.

United's secretary Mr J.J.Bentley, who held the post with Bolton for many years at the commencement of League football, held many reminiscences of the old days. His

The Great Lever End in 1914. These were exciting times for Wanderers with some memorable FA Cup games at Burnden. Alas, World War One was just around the corner.

stories included the free scoring during his connection with the Trotters and his mind must have gone vividly back to the time when sixes and sevens were not so uncommon.

The Wanderers, having had a week of sea breeze and fresh surroundings at Lytham, asserted themselves early on with Evan Jones striking the crossbar.

In the 26th minute George Lillycrop scored a beautiful goal that brought the house down. Jones broke through and beat both United backs before skilfully passing into the centre and as Beale came out, Lillycrop put the ball into the net.

Joe Smith got a second in the 38th minute, following up on a shot from Lillycrop that Beale had failed to hold.

Just before the interval, Smith headed Bolton's third, connecting on to Alec Donaldson's sweeping right-wing cross.

The Bolton supporters went wild with delight when Joe Smith capped a fine afternoon's performance by booking his first hat-trick in League football four minutes into the second half.

The Wanderers played brilliant football for a 20-minute spell their passing being so quick and effective the Reds could never judge them.

Jones beat Beale with a right-foot drive for The Trotters fifth in the 67th minute but almost immediately the old Notts inside forward West pulled one back for United when his effort hit the woodwork before cannoning into the net.

It was the result of smart work by Donaldson and Lillycrop that Smith was able to break all his own fine goalscoring records by shooting the Wanderers' sixth goal.

The directors were so pleased with the result that as a special acknowledgement the team were sent back to Lytham to prepare for the FA Cup-tie against Port Vale.

Bolton Wanderers: Edmondson; Stott, Feebury, Glendenning, Fay, Rowley, Donaldson, Jones, Lillycrop, Smith, Vizard.
Manchester United: Beale; Roberts, Hodge, Gipps, Knowles, Haywood, Meredith, Turnbull, Anderson, West, Wall.

Attendance: 32,306
Referee: S.D.Peers (Liverpool)

Southern Leaguers Beaten at Burnden
31 January 1914
BOLTON WANDERERS 4 SWINDON TOWN 2

At two o'clock, an hour before the start of this FA Cup second-round tie, there were 30,000 people, invading the slopes of Burnden like flies around a jar of jam. It wasn't everyday that they had the opportunity of seeing the leaders of the Southern League in Lancashire, hence the big crowd.

The Trotters had come home from Lytham as fit as fiddles and Swindon, victors over the Manchester United in the previous round, had trained on the breezy downs of Wiltshire.

Bolton's reception was a real hearty one and they turned out on a turf that looked ideal. It is not often that

spectators risk their necks by climbing on to the stays of the stands, but a few found vantage points there.

Swindon made the first raid on the left, but Baverstock broke up the move whilst Vizard was quickly cheered for an enterprising run.

After nine minutes of play the Swindon folk went crazy over an opening goal. From a corner by Jefferson, Batty, tall and strong, came romping through with a header that struck the crossbar and glanced into the net. The Wanderers did not have to wait long for an equaliser which came from an identical route. Donaldson's flag kick, as accurate as

Jefferson's, found Joe Smith's head that urged the ball into the net just inside the post.

Swindon began the second half like a house on fire, Joe Edmondson having to fist away a powerful drive from Bolland.

Twelve minutes into the second half the Wanderers won the lead with a goal by Smith. The inside man met Donaldson's centre and shot the ball past Skiller's despairing dive.

The Cup-tie was virtually secured when Bolton made it 4-1 in a 15-minute spell. Evans side-stepped a challenge and swished the ball high into the net, and then Smith completed his hat-trick when he tapped the ball into an empty goal after Donaldson's

attempt had come back off the crossbar.

The Swindon boys didn't give up and in the 73rd minute Batty scored their second goal with a well struck shot.

A third-round tie awaited the Trotters at Burnley where, unfortunately, Cup interest ended for another season.

Bolton Wanderers: Edmondson; Baverstock, Feebury, Glendenning, Fay, Rowley, Donaldson, Jones, Lillycrop, Smith, Vizard.
Swindon Town: Skiller; McRobbie, Giles, Tout, Silto, Handley, Jefferson, Batty, Wheatcroft, Bown, Bolland.

Attendance: 50,558
Referee: A.Denton (Leeds)

Bolton's playing squad of 1913-14, when they finished sixth in Division One. Back row (left to right): S.Gimblett, W.Jennings, J.Baverstock, J.Tyldesley, J.Edmondson, J.Thomas, S.Greenhalgh, J.Feebury. Middle row: G.Eccles (trainer), G.Cartwright, J.Cooke, J.Slater, R.Glendenning, J.Fay, W.Rowley, J.Bullough, E.Whiteside, H.Baverstock, W.Hughes, J.Sankey (assistant trainer). Front row: W.Scott, A.Donaldson, H.Hilton, A.Weir, E.Jones, G.Lillycrop, J.Smith, E.Vizard, W.Westwood, D.Stokes.

Wanderers' Wartime Misery
2 October 1915
BOLTON WANDERERS 0 SOUTHPORT CENTRAL 7

This was a result half expected by the brave spirits who patronised this Lancashire Section Principal competition match. In mitigation it may be said that the Southport side were one of the best in Lancashire and what is more they were practically all born in and around the town.

The main advantage in Southport's

favour was that most of their players had experience of First or Second Division football whereas the Wanderers had no such luxury. Indeed, the Southport captain was none other than Jimmy Fay who represented the Wanderers before the war and again after the hostilities ceased. A large military demonstration in the town, organised by the War Office, combined with a wretched drizzle, had the effect of reducing the crowd to next door to zero.

Bolton should have taken the lead early on when, from Rowley's pass, Gannon, with the goal at his mercy, hesitated so long as to lose a beautiful

Jimmy Fay, Southport's captain who returned to Burnden Park in 1917.

chance. After eight minutes play Southport went ahead, Potts shooting through a crowd of players from a right-wing corner.

The football was not without interest although it was marked by those little deficiencies that characterise players out of regular training.

Abrahams hit Southport's second in the 27th minute and it was becoming apparent that the Wanderers were no match for the visitors. They did well not to concede again before the interval.

Lightfoot and Potts doubled the advantage early in the second half and then a fast Southport movement led to a cross coming in from the left that was converted by Lightfoot.

Rigby netted a sixth, going through on his own, and from a Semple's centre Potts completed his hat-trick in what was his first appearance in Southport's colours.

Bolton Wanderers: Kay; Greenhalgh, Shipperbottom, Hothersall, Rowley, Entwistle, Waller, Gannon, Mather, Devitt, Gay.
Southport: Drabble; Dorward, Holborn, Holdsworth, Fay, Abrahams, Rigby, Caulfield, Lightfoot, Potts, Semple.

Attendance: 50
Referee: L.N.Fletcher (Bury)

Smith's Double Hat-trick Hits Stoke
23 September 1916
BOLTON WANDERERS 9 STOKE 2

Hundreds of wounded soldiers who watched this Lancashire Section Principal competition match were treated to a goal bonanza by a strong Bolton side that had failed to win any of its opening three games of the season. Stoke, on the other hand, were unbeaten but had a sample of what was to come when they fell behind after 30 seconds.

Buchan and Smith combined well to set up the opportunity for Sharp to hit

the net and they continued to create a number of chances early on.

It wasn't until the 20th minute, however, that Joe Smith had the gift of his first goal of the season thanks to a pin-point cross by Pickup.

Stoke hit back a minute later, Harrison slinging the ball into the middle for Bridgett to slice in and poke the ball past Hodgkiss.

The Wanderers went further ahead as the result of a centre by Sharp which dropped plumb on the crossbar. It rolled along the woodwork for a couple of yards but didn't go out of play and Vizard brought it back, hitting the opposite upright before seeing it cannon into the net.

The spectators were excited by this goal and had more to cheer about seconds later when Smith outwitted Turner and shot a typical left-foot goal after 27 minutes play.

Smith completed his hat-trick after 50 minutes. He put in a tremendous shot that full-back Twemlow turned over with his hand, the forward converting the penalty kick with such power that the referee went to check for any fractures in the netting, much to the amusement of the crowd.

Smith made it a half-dozen for Bolton with a shot from the edge of the penalty area and then Sharp converted a perfect centre from Vizard.

Smith hit the Wanderers' eighth goal from Pickup's cross yet the remarkable feature of all this scoring was that Stoke at times looked like holding their own.

Bridgett took the total goals tally into double figures by getting Stoke's second, but the last word went to Smith, who completed his double hat-trick from a pass so admirably worked by Vizard that it was impossible to miss.

Joe Smith, whose double hat-trick against Stoke is still the highest tally by a Wanderers player in an organised game.

Bolton Wanderers: Hodgkiss; Farnworth, Hurst, Hulme, Heslop, Buchan, Pickup, Sharp, Geddes, Smith, Vizard.
Stoke: Herron; Turner, Twemlow, Jones, Parker, Limen, Harrison, Herbert, Humphreys, Bridgett, Ellis.

Attendance: 2,116
Referee: R.McLachin (Stockport)

A Rare Christmas Box!

25 December 1920
BOLTON WANDERERS 6 SUNDERLAND 2

It was a disappointment to the large crowd for the Division One Christmas Day match that David Jack, the Wanderers' recent acquisition from Plymouth Argyle, did not appear, but this was tempered somewhat by the display of his stand-in Bruce Longworth.

It was natural that the young Longworth lacked some effectiveness in front of goal, but his passing was beautiful and Alec Donaldson reaped the rewards with great effect.

Jack had caught a severe cold and it would have been unwise for him to turn out under those circumstances, although the management regretted his absence in view of the announcement that he would play.

The Wanderers gave a crowd of over 40,000 spectators a rare Christmas box with Sunderland receiving the full

Frank Roberts who rounded off the half dozen for the Wanderers against Sunderland.

the hero was so dazed in heading a ball that must have been as heavy as lead, he had to be taken from the field apparently oblivious to the state of affairs.

The ground was terribly heavy and treacherous but the pace was amazingly fast and the footwork was as accurate as one could wish to see.

Sunderland's new 'keeper Dempster, signed from a Scottish junior club would not forget his first-ever visit to Burnden. Smith's cannonballs were absolutely unstoppable and these went towards his tally of 38 League goals during the term that remain a club record.

Frank Roberts rounded off the half dozen for the Wanderers who were to finish the season in third spot in Division One, a position never bettered.

Bolton Wanderers: Hughes; Baverstock, Jones, Seddon, Fay, T . B u c h a n , D o n a l d s o n , Longworth, Roberts, Smith, Vizard.

S u n d e r l a n d : D e m p s t e r ; Hobson, Young, Parker, Sherwin, Mitton, Travers, C . B u c h a n , Cooke, Moore, Martin.

weight of an unexpected avalanche in the final quarter of an hour when their defence collapsed like a pack of cards.

After Jimmy Seddon and Joe Smith had put Bolton into a comfortable position, the storm suddenly burst into the greatest fury when by sheer grit and perseverance Sunderland drew level with goals by Buchan and Moore.

It was principally due to Joe Smith, who recorded a hat-trick in the space of five minutes, that caused the air to become charged with excitement after the visitors had cast gloom over the crowd by their recovery.

Directly after scoring his last goal,

Right: Jimmy Seddon, who opened the scoring against Sunderland.

Attendance: 39,521
Referee: H.Mason (Birmingham)

A Burnden Welcome for Dick Pym

27 August 1921
BOLTON WANDERERS 2 PRESTON NORTH END 2

The Burnden Park First Division season opened with a great wave of enthusiasm, welcoming new goalkeeper Dick Pym who joined the club for a then record £5,000.

North End, who turned out in white which was theirs by right, were given a great reception but this was exceeded by the great cry which greeted Joe Smith and his team in blue.

The Trotters, facing the Town goal, opened on a high note, Vizard going away cleverly to make a cross which Hamilton headed away.

The defences in general successfully locked and barred the door, Pym twice had to fist away in difficult positions and the nearest promise to a score was when Jack rounded the Preston defence and Vizard shot wide.

There was only a minute to half-time when Quantrill dropped in a centre which Roberts collected. Pym dived at his feet but, owing to Hodson having intervened, knocked the ball against the North Ender and it cannoned back towards goal. It was an easy matter for Roberts to put the ball into the net to give Preston the lead.

Bolton were stung by the course of events and equalised early in the second half from the penalty spot. Herbert's right-wing cross was handled by Mercer in his attempt to clear and Smith converted the kick.

There was ten minutes remaining when Joe Smith set the Welkin ringing with a real old timer. The move started with Roberts who dribbled his way up the middle before playing out to Vizard.

Instead of driving in, he coolly waited for Smith to run on to the ball for a left-foot drive which flew into the net.

The Wanderers had found their feet at last but there was to be disappointment in the final seconds when North End equalised.

Quantrill put in a low shot which Pym touched away but, as the ball never rose, Roberts had no difficulty in racing in to level.

Dick Pym, who made his Bolton debut against Preston at Burnden Park, at the start of what was to prove a wonderful career for the Wanderers.

Bolton Wanderers: Pym; Elvey, Hodson, Longworth, Seddon, Jennings, Herbert, Jack, F.Roberts, Smith, Vizard.
Preston North End: Elliott; Hamilton, Doolan, Waddell, McAll, Mercer, Rawlings, Jeffries, W.Roberts, Woodhouse, Quantrill.

Attendance: 39,993
Referee: J.Davies (Rainhill)

David Jack Shows the Way
4 October 1922
THE FOOTBALL LEAGUE 5 THE IRISH LEAGUE 1

For the third time since the Wanderers became a force in football an Inter League Challenge match was played on their ground, this being the second at Burnden Park.

The Irish had never succeeded in defeating a Football League side and nobody expected the sequence to be broken in this encounter.

The fact that David Jack, the

Just after World War One, ladies football in the North-West flourished and, although Bolton Wanderers had no affiliation to the team, the Bolton Ladies were allowed to use Burnden Park for the occasional game. Many of the players had transferred their allegiance from the hockey game and Burnden Park saw them defeat Manchester on 27 December 1917. Dick, Kerr's (from Preston) on 27 April 1918, and in 1919 the Bolton team came out on top against Leigh. This photograph shows the Bolton Ladies team in 1921 at Burnden Park.

Opposite page: David Jack, who represented the Football League on his home ground and scored two goals against the Irish League.

Wanderers' inside-right, was in the home team, that Jimmy Seddon was first reserve and that George Eccles acted as trainer gave the game a local flavour.

On a fine and warm afternoon the Football League side kicked off towards the Embankment but it was the Irish who soon took the lead.

A shot from Dalrymple was charged down but the ball went back to McKenzie and he scored with a well placed drive high up into the far corner of the net.

From the restart the Football League went away to equalise at once. A beautiful pass by Dorrell sent Roberts away to cross the ball accurately to Jack and, with a powerful left-foot shot from just outside the area, the Wanderer beat Harland cleverly amid loud applause.

After 18 minutes Jack put in a cross shot which Harland never attempted to touch and so the Football League held the initiative. The Irish defenders stuck pluckily to their task although harassed by relentless pressure but they couldn't prevent Roberts dashing in for the Football League's third in the 22nd minute.

The Football League forwards could not be held and, from a swinging cross by Carr, Cross beat Harland for a fourth time.

Having strained a leg muscle Carr was unable to resume for the second half, reducing England to ten men.

Despite this set-back the home side continued to hold their own and 12 minutes from time Roberts scored a fifth.

Football League: Pearson (West Brom); Clay (Spurs), Maitland (South Shields), Kean (Sheffield Wednesday), Wadsworth (Liverpool), Mechan (Chelsea), Carr (Middlesbrough), Jack (Bolton), Roberts (Preston), Cross (Burnley), Dorrell (Aston Villa).

Irish League: Harland (Linfield); McLeod (Queen's Island), Frame (Linfield), Wallace (Linfield), Risk (Distillery), McIlveene (Linfield), McKenzie (Distillery), Croft (Queens Island), Dalrymple (Distillery), Baker (Distillery), Burns (Glenavon).

Attendance: 10,000

John Smith's Memorable Debut
25 November 1922
BOLTON WANDERERS 2 MANCHESTER CITY 1

Having gone down 2-0 in the First Division match against Manchester City at Hyde Road the previous weekend, the Wanderers were looking for a victory that would not only gain revenge, but would improve their lowly League position.

The final piece to what was to become an FA Cup winning side had been added during the week, John Smith coming to Burnden from Glasgow Rangers for a £3,000 fee.

He lined up against City to make his debut, although the Wanderers were without Jimmy Seddon, injured in the previous week's game, and Billy Butler who was suffering from flu.

John Smith, signed from Glasgow Rangers and scored the winner against Manchester City on his debut.

Former Bolton centre-forward Frank Roberts lined up for City, having left Burnden the previous month after he had taken over the management of licenced premises, which was against club rules.

The Wanderers, who had done most of the early attacking, went ahead after 29 minutes play. Joe Smith was brought down in full flight 25 yards from goal. The captain took the kick, but instead of trying to crash it home with his usual ferocity he merely pushed it aside for David Jack to send it into the net.

A minute from half-time City were given a gift of an equaliser when Howarth appeared to take the ball from Pym's hands leaving Barnes the simple task of pushing the ball through.

The Wanderers lost Billy Jennings through injury early after the restart, Joe Smith falling back to left-half.

The game was very open and quick as a flash play travelled back and forth. Five minutes from time, in a fierce rally by Bolton, Vizard hooked the ball through but for some unseen infringement the referee disallowed the point much to the annoyance of the crowd.

They did not have long to wait to see what turned out to be the Wanderers' legitimate winner.

Vizard broke away down the left, and though harassed he turned a centre into the goalmouth and with Goodchild engaged elsewhere, John Smith headed into the net amidst tremendous enthusiasm.

Bolton Wanderers: Pym; Haworth, Finney,

Nuttall, Rowley, Jennings, E.Roberts, Jack, J.R.Smith, J.Smith, Vizard.
Manchester City: Goodchild; Cookson, Allen, Sharp, Hamill, Pringle, Morris, F.Roberts, Johnson, Barnes, Murphy.

Attendance: 28,611
Referee: F.Cheetham (Preston)

(Top): Joe Smith leads the Wanderers out at Burnden along with the side's mascots.

(Bottom): The first Wembley winners and FA Cup winners for the first time in the club's history. A line up on the Burnden mud in 1923. From left to right are Eccles (trainer), Seddon, Pym, Rowley, Finney, Jennings, Jack, Vizard, Nuttall (who was born in the house just visible behind the stand), John Smith, Haworth, Butler and Joe Smith.

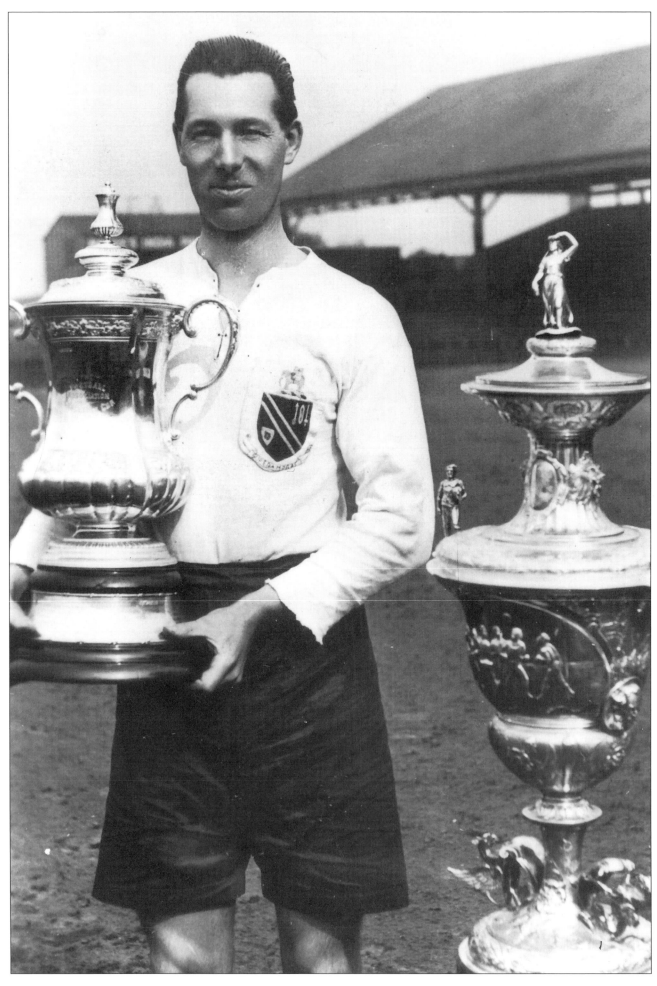

The Lancashire Cup Comes to Burnden

21 January 1925
BOLTON WANDERERS 2 BLACKPOOL 1

The Wanderers met Blackpool in the Final of the Lancashire Cup having won the toss for choice of ground.

Bolton were unchanged from their League side that had won at Notts County the previous Saturday with the exception that Billy Jennings who, in his long career, had never won a Lancashire Cup medal, came in at left-half for Nelson Howarth.

Blackpool were unchanged from their previous League encounter and they kicked off on a dull Wednesday afternoon.

The Wanderers wore red and white stripes in an attempt to familiarise themselves with the kit for their forthcoming FA Cup visit to Tottenham Hotspur.

The visitors set a merry pace and during the first five minutes exerted such pressure that Bolton's defenders were apt to get flurried. There was a slight improvement just before the interval but they were a long way removed from the side that had performed so well in the last game.

Bolton commenced the second half with only ten men, Harry Greenhalgh being absent through injury, although he was later to return. The Seasiders went ahead in the 77th minute, a pass back towards goal by Jennings went straight to Streets and he got to the ball before Finney to put the ball into the net.

The Wanderers then attacked in great desperation and equalised with six minutes remaining. David Jack collected a loose ball after an enterprising run by Butler to shoot past Crompton.

Just before time a corner from Vizard fell to Nuttall and he found the net with a glorious long shot to secure the trophy.

It was a dramatic victory, the reward of a great recovery after all had seemed lost.

Bolton Wanderers: Pym; Greenhalgh, Finney, Nuttall, Seddon, Jennings, Butler, D.Jack, Cassidy, Smith, Vizard.
Blackpool: Crompton; Leaver, Jones, Watson, Curran, Benton, Meredith, Streets, Bedford, Barrass, Mee.

Attendance: 11,292
Referee: F.Slater (Blackburn)

Rovers Have no Answer to Jack

22 April 1925
BOLTON WANDERERS 6 BLACKBURN ROVERS 0

The Wanderers were in rampant mood for this rearranged evening First Division fixture with near neighbours from Ewood Park. David Jack sent most of the 14,000 spectators away from Burnden Park delighted by getting four of the six goals which overwhelmed Rovers.

This was Bolton's 16th League win at home, yet on their travels they had managed only four successes. This had proved enough to put them into the championship race and, although the title went to Huddersfield, this demolition of Blackburn left them requiring two wins from as many games to secure their best ever spot of runners-up.

Yet another home win was registered three days later, this time against Liverpool, but the away form again cost the club when they returned from West Brom with only a point and had to settle for third place.

Jack's four goals against Rovers was enough to earn him the mantle of being the Wanderers' leading League

Opposite page:
Ted Vizard proudly shows off the FA Cup and stands alongside the much more impressive Lancashire Cup.

Joe Smith and Ted Vizard – the international left-wing pair who helped the Wanderers to third place in Division One during 1924-25.

goalgetter with a total of 26, a couple more than Joe Smith.

Jack was credited with his sides first, second, fourth and sixth goals whilst John Smith got the third and Joe Smith the fifth.

The Rovers were almost played to a standstill, Bolton being heaven at every turn and the score might have assumed double figures if the Trotters had desired to keep up the pace they set.

Jack was the most elusive player and probably turned in his best game of the campaign, his shooting being wonderfully accurate. On this performance he would surely add to his England international tally of two caps.

Rovers' new 'keeper, Crawford, had a very warm introduction to English League football, blundering before Jack obtained the first goal, although he made amends afterwards by the confidence he displayed in preventing a further avalanche.

Bolton Wanderers: Pym; Howarth, Greenhalgh, Nuttall, Seddon, Jennings, Boston, D.Jack, J.R.Smith, J.Smith, Vizard.
Blackburn Rovers: Crawford; Hope, Rollo, Roscamp, Pool, Campbell, Hulme, McCleery, Puddefoot, McKay, Holland.

Attendance: 14,000
Referee: T.Crewe (Leicester)

Bolton's Ten Men Assure no Cup Upset

9 January 1926
BOLTON WANDERERS 1 ACCRINGTON STANLEY 0

After having secured the FA Cup in 1923, the Wanderers had made exits from the competition in successive seasons on home territory and they were leaving nothing to chance in this third-round tie against Accrington.

Indeed, the underdogs had already given up home territory, the tie being switched to Burnden in the interests of safety with Accrington's ground capable of holding only 12,000 spectators.

The Wanderers almost took the lead inside ten minutes, a fierce shot from Butler striking the head of Kasher with goalkeeper Holden well beaten.

Accrington began to fight with great vigour and enthusiasm, Pym having to go down well to save a shot from Rooks.

Towards the interval the game became quite heated and it appeared as if a Stanley defender had handled in the area, the referee turning away the frantic appeals.

Bolton commenced the second half in much brighter fashion. After Joe Smith had brought Holden to his knees and Butler had shot many yards over the bar though well placed, Jack ran through four minutes after the restart to open the scoring.

There was a sensation six minutes later when, after a long consultation with the linesman, the referee ordered Vizard off the field for an alleged offence against Field. There had been a hot duel between the pair and the referee had penalised Field for an apparent trip when there was another scene before the referee took his drastic action, much to the consternation of the crowd.

The game became very fierce after this incident, Gee receiving a lecture and the nerves of the other players being on a knife-edge.

The visitors began to show signs of wear and tear and despite being a player to the good never seriously threatened the Bolton goal.

At the end of the game the police had to escort the officials, not only to the safety of the dressing-rooms, but on to their trains, such was the anger of the crowd at the dismissal of Vizard for the first time in his career.

It was an eventful start to what was to be a successful Cup journey.

Bolton Wanderers: Pym; Howarth, Jennings, Cope, Seddon, Thornborough, Butler, Jack, J.R.Smith, J.Smith, Vizard.
Accrington Stanley: Holden; Bell, Whittaker, Field, Kasher, Rooks, Wyper, Gee, Jepson, Powell, Gummery.

Attendance: 32,875
Referee: A.Ward (Kirkham)

Joe Smith's Swan-song
1 January 1927
BOLTON WANDERERS 2 LIVERPOOL 1

The Wanderers and Liverpool both turned out below strength on their return First Division match at Burnden, the Anfield side having won 3-2 on their home patch three days earlier.

Seddon, with an injured foot, and Vizard, not fully recovered from an attack of influenza, were out of the Wanderers side. Thornborough got his chance for his first appearance of the season in an unaccustomed position of centre-half.

Liverpool were in an even worse plight for they had both their backs

disabled and gave League debuts to Pither and Done.

In honour of his benefit, Butler captained the Wanderers team and from the kick-off immediately won a free-kick in a dangerous position. Nuttall placed the ball well forward for Jack to sprint in and fail by the narrowest of margins to catch the ball close to the upright.

For a time the Liverpool defence was hard pressed, the Trotters showing excellent ball control and McKinlay's head twice getting to the ball in the nick of time as Jack made an effort to rush it through.

A perfect centre by Jack brought the Wanderers a well deserved reward, John Smith trapping the ball right in front of goal and beating Scott with a fast rising shot after withstanding a charge by Done.

Against the run of play in the 36th minute, Edmed made a surprise long shot from the wing to equalise the score for Liverpool. It was a case of drawing a bow at a venture and it coming off.

During the second half the Wanderers almost became non-existent as a shooting force, only David Jack showing any marked initiative in opening out an attack.

The Wanderers began to brighten up towards the end, Jack having a clever attempt to scramble the ball into the net cleared by Scott.

Six minutes from time John Smith gave his side the lead with a shot from

close range which Scott partially stopped but couldn't prevent from rolling over the line.

Unbeknown to the crowd of the time, this was to be the end of an era with Joe Smith playing his last League game for the club, his 449 appearances having produced 254 goals.

Bolton Wanderers: Pym; Greenhalgh, Finney, Cope, Thornborough, Nuttall, Butler, Jack, J.R.Smith, J.Smith, Picken.
Liverpool: Scott; Done, McKinlay, McNab, Pratt, Bromilow, Edmed, Hodgson, Baron, Chambers, Pither.
Attendance: 34,513
Referee: R.Bowie (Newcastle upon Tyne)

Bolton Wanderers in 1926-27. Back row (left to right): Cope, Greenhalgh, Pym, Seddon, Nuttall. Front row: Butler, Jack, J.R.Smith, Baggett, Vizard, Finney. Inset: Joe Smith.

McClelland Makes his Mark on Burnden Debut
24 March 1928
BOLTON WANDERERS 3 LEICESTER CITY 3

Jim McClelland's introduction to the Burnden Park football public was the main feature of Leicester City's visit for this First Division match.

The Scotsman, who had signed from Middlesbrough, made his debut a week earlier, scoring in a 2-2 draw at Burnley. Ted Vizard also returned to the side having been missing through injury since early January.

This was to be one of the best games of the season at Burnden as individualism found full expression and yet team work was there too. The result was a charming display of football which the crowd frankly revelled in.

The Trotters made most of the early running, Gibson vying with Jack, as a maker of openings. Both the Scot and his partner were unfairly brought down near the corner flag but Vizard's free-kicks were well covered.

Such pressure as the Wanderers were exerting was bound to tell and in the 26th minute, brilliant dribbling by Gibson brought a through pass to

Burnden Park from the corner of the Great Lever/Darcy Lever end of the ground.

McClelland so beautifully timed that he was out on his own when he collected the ball. Running a few yards he made no mistake with a hard shot into the corner of the net.

Five minutes from half-time Vizard's centre was missed by both Jack and McClelland but Butler was on hand to ram the ball home for Bolton's second.

The referee was playing injury time when Adcock's brilliant run brought a pass to Hine which was taken on the run and slammed past Gough for the visitors' opener.

The second half saw a couple of goals inside four minutes. First Chandler equalised for Leicester, netting as Nuttall rushed in to tackle him, then the Wanderers regained the advantage with McClelland heading Butler's pin-point centre past McLaren.

Leicester came back again but it wasn't until 16 minutes from time that Hine got in an accurate shot that earned his side a point.

The only fault that could be pointed at the Bolton defence was Nuttall's rather weak kicking which was a blot on an otherwise clever game by the international.

Bolton Wanderers: Gough; Nuttall, Jennings, Cope, Seddon, Wright, Butler, Jack, McClelland, Gibson, Vizard.
Leicester City: McLaren; Black, Brown, Duncan, Carr, Bishop, Adcock, Hine, Chandler, Lochhead, Barry.

Attendance: 18,142
Referee: A.J.Prince-Cox (London)

Wanderers Settle Cup-tie in Extra-time
30 January 1929
BOLTON WANDERERS 5 LIVERPOOL 2 (AFTER EXTRA-TIME)

There was a resurgence of the old wave of enthusiasm which was created when the Wanderers won the FA Cup in 1923 and 1926 for the visit of Liverpool for this FA Cup fourth-round replay.

Half an hour before the start more than 20,000 had passed through the 56 turnstiles and there seemed as many more outside.

Both sides received a rousing reception and it was a tense moment as 40,000 people stood bareheaded and heartily sang the National Anthem.

The Wanderers kicked off towards the Great Lever goal but it was Dick

Pym who was first called into action when he had to turn a long left-foot shot from Clark over the bar.

First one goal then the other was attacked in such a way as to keep the crowd in a continual state of excitement.

At the end of 33 minutes Lindsay placed in a shot which Pym reached under the bar but couldn't hold and it dropped behind him into the net.

Liverpool's joy was short-lived as within three minutes McClelland had pounced on a cross from Kean to hit a low left-foot drive into the goal.

The Wanderers side that secured the FA Cup for the third time in 1929. Back row (left to right): Kean, Haworth, Pym, Finney, Nuttall. Front row: Butler, McClelland, Seddon, Blackmore, Gibson, Cook.

The crowd then went wild when Bolton went ahead, Gibson running across the goalmouth before turning quickly to leave Ripley helpless.

After the scoreless draw between the sides on the previous Saturday, this tie was making up for the lack of goals in that game and Liverpool equalised in the 65th minute. Clark broke through for the Anfielders and set up Hodgson, who appeared to be in an offside position, to hit the ball inside the upright.

The game was desperately fought to the end and there was nothing for it but to play a further half an hour.

Bolton grabbed the initiative after six minutes, Blackmore taking a Butler centre in his stride to smash a magnificent shot into the net.

Some of the players could scarcely raise a gallop but Butler put the Wanderers further ahead with a well-placed corner that Ripley could only help into the net.

In the closing stages, Blackmore scored a fifth to earn the Wanderers a fifth-round tie at Leicester City in what was to be another Cup winning season.

Bolton Wanderers: Pym; Haworth, Finney, Kean, Seddon, Nuttall, Butler, McClelland, Blackmore, Gibson, Cook.
Liverpool: Ripley; Jackson, Done, Morrison, Davidson, Bromilow, Edmed, Clark, Hodgson, McDougall, Lindsay.

Attendance: 41,808
Referee: A.Josephs (South Shields)

Trotters Open New Year with Seven Goals
1 January 1930
BOLTON WANDERERS 7 HUDDERSFIELD TOWN 1

Huddersfield Town's visit to Burnden constituted an attractive New Year's Day First Division fixture for the Wanderers and even the bad weather failed to affect the attendance.

Jimmy Seddon returned to the

Billy Butler hit a hat-trick against Huddersfield Town during a 7-1 New Year's Day victory.

Below: The familiar railway bridge over Manchester Road outside Burnden Park, pictured in 1930.

Wanderers side to bring them back to full strength, the Yorkshire club looking to gain revenge for a 2-0 reverse at Leeds Road 11 days earlier.

Since then Town had won three games, two away from home, Wanderers also being unbeaten with a 5-0 trouncing of E v e r t o n rounding off 1929.

Despite an early kick-off the crowd rolled up in good spirits and had to wait only six minutes for Bolton to go ahead.

From Cook's centre the ball ran to Butler's toe and he hit it first time against the underside of the Great Lever goal.

A stoppage occurred when Nuttall was knocked out in heading the heavy ball but he quickly resumed and it was in keeping with the play that the Wanderers went further ahead in the 19th minute.

Again from a centre by Cook, both friend and foe jumped to head it and, as it dropped on the fringe of the crowd, Butler drove it hard against the inside of the upright and into the net.

Butler completed his hat-trick after 23 minutes, rushing in to divert Cook's cross out of Turner's reach. Some idea of the extent to which Huddersfield had been subdued was gathered from the fact that in half an hour Pym did not have to make a single save.

Four minutes after the interval Mangnall capitalised on a defensive error to put Town back in the game but Cook restored the advantage for Bolton three minutes later.

In the next Bolton attack Blackmore beat Turner with a high cross shot and he then made it three goals for Bolton in the space of four minutes with a goal from 18 yards out.

Gibson rounded off the scoring for the Wanderers with a simple seventh but, after this game, the side found goals difficult to come by, scoring only seven in as many games.

Bolton Wanderers: Pym; Haworth, Finney, Kean, Seddon, Nuttall, Butler, McKay, Blackmore, Gibson, Cook.
Huddersfield Town: Turner; Goodall, Spence, Fogg, Wilson, Campbell, G.Kelly, R.Kelly, Mangnall, Raw, Smith.

Attendance: 27,355
Referee: R.Brown (Newcastle upon Tyne)

Ray Westwood Makes his Burnden Bow
28 March 1931
BOLTON WANDERERS 1 MANCHESTER CITY 1

For the First Division fixture against Manchester City at Burnden the Wanderers brought back goalkeeper Bob Jones and centre-half Jimmy Seddon and gave a debut to Ray Westwood.

Westwood, an 18-year-old Brierley Hill forward, came to Burnden Park on the recommendation of former Wanderers David Stokes and Jack Round. Having played for both Stourbridge and Brierley Hill Alliance he had trials with Aston Villa that came to nothing and this was his big chance.

Westwood replaced the evergreen Ted Vizard whose first-team career now came to an end at almost 42 years of age.

Blackmore kicked off and he was soon responsible for a neat header which Barnett intercepted. Facing a stiff breeze the Wanderers were pressed for space.

City became rather more assertive, although Blackmore and Butler made two dangerous rushes which demanded intervention by the City defenders. The West Countryman then enthused the crowd by rounding Cowan and flashing a drive inches over.

After 14 minutes a basic mistake by Finney gave City a rather fortunate lead. The Bolton back intercepted a pass from Halliday and, with plenty of time to clear, missed his kick and Brook darted in to shoot past Jones.

The Wanderers played hard and there were grounds for their penalty claim during a mass attack on the City goal when Cowan appeared to knock down a shot by McKay.

The referee, having none of it, checked with the linesman who agreed with him.

City's goal then led a charmed life and, during an exciting spell, Blackmore drove in a ball which again Cowan fouled with his hand. A penalty was given without hesitation and Blackmore converted the kick to equalise after 37 minutes.

The second half saw another Bolton penalty appeal turned away and Wrightson shoot wide of an open goal for City in the final minute.

One of the happiest features of the game was the form of the young Westwood who combined well with Gibson, especially after the interval.

Bolton Wanderers: Jones; Wagstaffe, Finney, Goslin, Seddon, Wright, Butler, McKay, Blackmore, Gibson, Westwood.
Manchester City: Langford; Ridley, Barnett, Busby, Cowan, McMillan, Toseland, Marshall, Halliday, Wrightson, Brook.
Attendance: 17,398
Referee: R.Brown (Newcastle upon Tyne)

Season Ends on a High Note
7 May 1932
BOLTON WANDERERS 8 LIVERPOOL 1

Liverpool's visit to Burnden Park marked the close of the Wanderers' First Division programme without any special significance, except for the first appearance of Dick Edmed, who made his Bolton debut against his old club.

Liverpool, who were without Gordon Hodgson who was on cricket duty, had six Scots in their side and were looking for revenge after losing 8-1 at Burnden earlier in the season in a third-round Lancashire Cup-tie.

It would have been interesting to see what the odds were on Bolton repeating that feat.

The Wanderers were one up inside 30 seconds, Jack Milsom working home a centre by Billy Cook, and they then put on two more by the seventh minute.

Milsom hit an unstoppable shot past Riley which went just inside the angle of the bar and post, then Edmed got into the act to score against his former club.

The goal glut continued when McRorie pulled one back for Liverpool in the ninth minute but things then quietened down until the 51st minute.

Then, Ray Westwood, who had an earlier effort ruled out for handball, set up Milsom to head home and complete his hat-trick. Milsom was on hand to register the Wanderers' fifth when he

was put clear to dribble round Riley and put the ball into an empty net.

Westwood fought off challenges from Bradshaw and Steel to hit the sixth before Fred Wilson struck what was to be his only League goal to make it 7-1.

The rout was completed when Westwood got a rare headed goal from Milsom's cross with Liverpool's defence in a bewildered state.

The Wanderers could have gone into double figures without exaggeration but a small Burnden crowd were more than pleased to end a difficult season on a high note.

The following week the Lancashire Cup was secured with a 3-2 win over Manchester City at Maine Road to put some silverware into the club's cabinet.

Bolton Wanderers: Jones; Duckworth, Finney, McKay, Griffiths, Howarth, Edmed, Wilson, Milsom, Westwood, Cook.
Liverpool: Riley; Steel, Done, Morrison, Bradshaw, McDougall, McRorie, Hancock, Wright, McPherson, Gunson.
Attendance: 9,209
Referee: I.Caswell (Blackburn)

Jack Milsom, who scored four goals in Bolton's 8-1 defeat of Liverpool on the final day of the 1931-32 season.

FA Cup Run Ends Before Burnden's Best Gate
18 February 1933
BOLTON WANDERERS 2 MANCHESTER CITY 4

Without a League win in eight games the Wanderers fielded an experimental side for their FA Cup fifth-round match against Manchester City, in front of what was to be the largest-ever attendance at Burnden Park.

Billy Butler returned to the side, after injury, to partner Dick Edmed on the right wing for the first time. This game was to be a test for Edmed who had been playing a lot of West Lancashire League football. Tonge full-back Tom Duckworth returned to the senior side for the first time since the previous September and goalkeeper Harry Church was taking part in his first FA Cup-tie.

City, who arrived only half an hour before the kick-off due to traffic congestion, held the early initiative but Bolton gradually got into their stride and Ray Westwood shaved the post with a header after 22 minutes.

A minute later the Wanderers went ahead, Edmed and Butler combining to get the ball into the goalmouth where Jack Milsom hooked through in fine style.

City equalised in the 31st minute, Brook ramming home a loose ball, and then, seconds later, Brook came from nowhere to send an oblique low shot past Church.

Bolton battled hard to get back on level terms and equalised after 57 minutes when Westwood found the net directly from a corner.

The turning point of the game came

Some of Burnden's best-ever attendance use any vantage point possible. Here they climb on to the roof of the Great Lever End and the refreshment hut. Alas, they saw their side go down 4-2 to Manchester City.

when City won a penalty, awarded after full-back Finney had handled, Brook stepping up to complete his hat-trick.

A late goal from Tilson gave City some breathing space although Milsom threw away a great chance when he shot at Langford with two colleagues waiting unmarked for a pass.

In the end it was City's more thrustful attack that won them the day.

Burnden Park saw another record four days later, a crowd of only 3,101 attended a First Division game against Portsmouth, this being the smallest for a League fixture until November 1985.

Bolton Wanderers: Church; Duckworth, Finney, Goslin, Griffiths, Howarth, Edmed, Butler, Milsom, Gibson, Westwood.
Manchester City: Langford; Cann, Dale, Busby, Cowan, Bray, Toseland, Marshall, Tilson, Herd, Brook.
Attendance: 69,912
Referee: H.E.Hull (Burnley)

Five Goals, but Relegation Looms

6 May 1933

BOLTON WANDERERS 5 LEEDS UNITED 0

The Wanderers were relegated for the fifth time, going down to the Second Division along with Blackpool, as rivals Wolves and Leicester both won.

Victory over Leeds United was imperative for Bolton to have any hope of avoiding the drop and they did all they could before events elsewhere overtook them.

The Wanderers left plenty of room for doubt with their finishing in the early states of the game. The deadlock was broken when McKay and Westwood combined to put Jack Milsom in possession and he hit the back of the net with a low shot.

Six minutes from half-time Milsom headed home Butler's cross and then the winger missed a glorious chance with an open goal at his mercy.

Milsom completed his hat-trick seconds from the interval with Butler

again being the provider. A great cheer went up when the latest scores were posted showing Wolves losing at home to Everton but they were to finally win 4-2.

Bolton continued to dominate Leeds and increased their lead in the 66th minute. Goalkeeper Moore failed to hold on to a Milsom rocket and Ray Westwood dashed in to hit the fourth.

Eight minutes from time Rimmer set up Westwood for what was to be the club's last First Division goal for two seasons.

In the final minute McKay hit the Leeds post and before the danger was cleared Butler lobbed a short centre to

Milsom who missed the goal from point-blank range.

The crowd laughed, they felt they could afford to. Unfortunately, the humour died down when the realisation that a spell of 22 years in the top flight had come to an end.

Bolton Wanderers: Church; Smith, Finney, Nicholson, Atkinson, Howarth, Butler, McKay, Milsom, Westwood, Rimmer.
Leeds United: Moore, G.W.Milburn, J.Milburn, Edwards, Hornby, Copping, Suggan, Hydes, Keetley, Furness, Mahon.

Attendance: 10,048
Referee: E.Wood (Sheffield)

The Bolton side of 1932-33 when they were relegated to Division Two. Back row (left to right): Bob Young (trainer), H.Goslin, J.Griffiths, H.Church, A.Finney, W.McKay, T.Griffiths. Front row: W.Butler, G.Gibson, J.Milsom, R.Westwood, W.Cook.

Trotters hit Eight in Record League Win

6 October 1934
BOLTON WANDERERS 8 BARNSLEY 0

An incredible spell of five goals in the final six minutes of this Second Division match was to take the Wanderers to their record League victory.

It was Barnsley's first visit to Burnden for 23 years, the Yorkshire

side having won the Third Division North championship the previous season and now holding their own in higher company during this term.

Steady rain was falling when Barnsley kicked off and they proceeded to win the first corner of the game.

Two of Ray
Westwood's
goals during
the Wanderers
record 8-0
League defeat
of Barnsley.

The opening goal came in the 21st minute, Eastham and Cook combining for the latter to centre to Westwood who slipped a side-footer inside the near post.

Twelve minutes later the Wanderers went two up, George Taylor's free-kick being a perfect length for Westwood to send in a flashing header.

Westwood went on to complete his hat-trick six minutes from half-time when he converted a pass from Milsom.

The more play went on the more evident it became that Barnsley were being outmatched by the Wanderers but they couldn't increase their lead.

The floodgates finally began to open in the 84th minute when G.T.Taylor made a chance for himself by cutting into the middle and winding up with an unstoppable shot.

Three minutes later Taylor got Bolton's fifth, converting a centre from Cook that entered the net off the post.

In the next attack Westwood broke through the middle and his effort was kicked into his own goal by Shotton.

To add to a sensational climax Westwood made an identical run and on this occasion found the net himself by rounding Ellis and slipping the ball into an empty net.

Just before the final whistle blew Westwood sent Milsom through to score a glorious eighth. The match ended in scenes of remarkable enthusiasm. Burnden's crowd rose to the Bolton players as they left the field, the result taking them to the top of the Second Division after they had won eight of their opening nine games.

Bolton Wanderers: Jones, R.Smith, Finney, Goslin, Atkinson, G.Taylor, G.T.Taylor, Eastham, Milsom, Westwood, Cook.
Barnsley: Ellis; Adey, Shotton, Harper, Henderson, Whitworth, Ashton, J.Smith, Finnigan, Andrews, Pedivers.

Attendance: 15,009
Referee: W.R.Jennings (York)

Defeat of Champions Makes Promotion Imminent

1 May 1935
BOLTON WANDERERS 2 BRENTFORD 0

The Wanderers needed nothing less than two points in this final Second Division home game of the season to take a firm hold on the runners-up spot.

On the other hand even partial success for Brentford, who had already been crowned champions and had not suffered a League reverse for three months, would strengthen West Ham's chance of pipping the Wanderers to promotion.

In the early stages Bolton were completely outplayed by faster and more methodical opponents. After Smith had twice stopped the Bees in full flight for goal, Hopkins raced away and shot hard into the side of the net when he had Jones completely at his mercy.

The Wanderers went ahead against the run of play in the 33rd minute. A good run by Westwood, who left two opponents standing, saw the ball pushed out to Cook who promptly lobbed it high into the goalmouth for Milsom to head it down to the foot of the post.

Mathieson promptly fell on the ball as it lay on the goal-line and, with half a dozen players on top of the 'keeper, the ball was scrambled away on the wrong side of the post. The referee, however, had already awarded a goal with the linesman also pointing to the centre.

Although the Brentford players surrounded the referee and protested strenuously he adhered to his decision.

The Londoners began to wane after this incident and the Wanderers went two up five minutes from half-time.

Mathieson dropped a Cook corner and, as Bateman attempted to clear, G.T.Taylor sailed in and drove the ball high into the roof of the net.

The second half object for Bolton was to hold what they had with Walton playing rather deeper to give assistance to the half-backs.

Burnden's best League attendance of the season saw a lacklustre second half but were happy in the knowledge that a point from a visit to Blackpool three days later would complete the job.

A Ray Westwood goal, his 30th of the season, earned a 1-1 draw and a return to the top flight.

Bolton Wanderers: Jones; Goldsmith, Smith, Goslin, Atkinson, G.Taylor, G.T.Taylor, Walton, Milsom, Westwood, Cook.
Brentford: Mathieson; Bateman, Poyser, McKenzie, James, Watson, Hopkins, Robson, Holliday, Scott, Fletcher.

Attendance: 46,554
Referee: B.C.White (Nuneaton)

The Bolton side that won promotion as runners-up to Brentford, pictured on a frosty Burnden Park in 1934-35. Back row (left to right): H.Goslin, J.Atkinson, R.Smith, R.Jones, A.Finney, G.Taylor. Front row: G.T.Taylor, G.Eastham, J.Milsom, R.Westwood, W.Cook. That season the Wanderers also reached the FA Cup semi-finals.

Trotters' Cup hopes Crumble at City's Hands
20 February 1937
BOLTON WANDERERS 0 MANCHESTER CITY 5

Another huge Burnden crowd of over 60,000 attended this FA Cup fifth-round tie to see if the Wanderers could avenge the defeat of 1933.

Harry Goslin during preseason training in the summer of 1936, and *opposite page* is George Eastham.

Bolton, however, were finding goals hard to come by and had not won a League game in ten attempts which had plunged them into a relegation battle.

The Wanderers attacked the Great Lever End in damp conditions and there were thrills straight away – Swift saving from a Milsom back header.

Alf Anderson – recruited from Hibernian – hits his first League goal during a 2-1 home reverse against Wolves in February 1937. Two weeks later he was in the side hammered 5-0 at Burnden in the FA Cup.

City's defence was hard worked and it was five minutes before Toseland threatened the Bolton goal.

Some luck and good goalkeeping was saving City with the Milsom and Westwood combination well on top.

Five minutes from half-time City took the lead somewhat against the run of play when Doherty ran through to set up Tilson for an easy short-range goal.

Eastham hit the inside of the post early in the second half but City went 2-0 up in the 59th minute when Herd pasted the ball into the net from what appeared to be an offside position. Bolton protested but it was all in vain, even though the referee consulted his linesman.

Things got out of hand on the field when Toseland and Anderson were involved in a fracas with the referee sending the Trotters' Scottish winger off the field.

Tennant was then nastily fouled by Doherty and the whole Bolton side demanded the offender's dismissal. The only result was a free-kick, and although Atkinson appeared to be attempting to persuade his colleagues to leave the field, wiser councils fortunately prevailed.

Brook hit City's third goal with a free-kick from just outside the area and with a minute remaining Herd headed home Brooks centre for the fourth.

Eastham, resenting another poor refereeing decision, kicked the ball into the Embankment and the crowd refused to return it. In time added on, Doherty made it 5-0 with a close-range effort.

At the final whistle, a strong body of police was required to escort the referee from the field whilst the grandstand spectators stood and voiced their disapproval of his performance.

Bolton Wanderers: Jones; Tennant, Connor, Goslin, Atkinson, G.Taylor, G.T.Taylor, Eastham, Milsom, Westwood, Anderson.
Manchester City: Swift; Dale, Barkas, Percival, Marshall, Bray, Toseland, Herd, Tilson, Doherty, Brook.

Attendance: 60,979
Referee: Captain G.Hamilton-Jones (Woolwich)

Honours Shared in Ten-goal Thriller
30 October 1937
BOLTON WANDERERS 5 CHELSEA 5

The Wanderers were without regular centre-forward Jack Milsom for their First Division match against Chelsea, his place being taken by Scottish striker Jack Calder.

In the last home game Preston had taken the points in a 4-1 win and the Wanderers' supporters were looking for some improvement.

Drizzling rain and poor light welcomed the sides as Calder kicked off. Anderson and Westwood combined well twice, one shot going narrowly wide and the other forcing a corner which came to nothing.

It was all Bolton for the opening five minutes, then Mills got away to send a square ground pass across goal and Chitty was on hand to put Chelsea one up.

Ray Westwood then took command, equalising when he received a pass from Anderson before bringing the ball down to shoot fiercely to the left of the goal.

Six minutes later the same combination culminated with a right-foot shot that crept inside the post to bring the house down.

Chelsea showed plenty of class football and deservedly equalised when Swift couldn't prevent a powerful shot from Argue hitting the net.

The second half began with two goals in as many minutes. Calder restored the Wanderers lead when he thrust a free-kick from Hurst past Woodley but, almost immediately, the Londoners were level with Argue converting a cross from Chitty.

Argue then put Chelsea ahead, completing his hat-trick, when Wanderers' 'keeper Frank Swift, misjudged a cross. Westwood, not to be outdone, then completed his hat-trick, converting a pass from Calder.

It was anybody's game in the last lap. Tom Grosvenor missed with a cross shot but ten minutes from time had the satisfaction of putting the Wanderers in front with a volley from the edge of the box.

There were only five minutes remaining when Mills cleverly converted Argue's headed pass to earn Chelsea a point from this remarkable thriller.

Bolton Wanderers: Swift; Tennant, Connor, Goslin, Atkinson, Hurst, Carruthers, Grosvenor, Calder, Westwood, Anderson.
Chelsea: Woodley; O'Hare, Barber, Mitchell, Griffiths, Miller, Buchanan, Argue, Mills, Burgess, Chitty.

Attendance: 22,293
Referee: E.C.Cornwell (Lichfield)

Jim Calder found the net in the remarkable 5-5 draw with Chelsea.

Hunt Helps Wanderers Defeat Throstles
19 March 1938
BOLTON WANDERERS 3 WEST BROMWICH ALBION 0

After only one win in the previous seven First Division games, the main pre-match highlight was the debut of George Hunt who had joined the Wanderers from Arsenal.

Earlier in the season Bolton had won 4-2 at The Hawthorns and they got off to a good start when, after six minutes Hunt began to repay some of his fee with an excellent opening goal.

The move began in the middle when Hunt passed to Westwood who dribbled forward and sent the ball straight between the full-backs as he was brought down. It looked to be Adams' ball but Hunt got there first and placed it past the 'keeper with the first shot of the game.

West Brom had penalty appeals turned away after Hubbick had appeared to handle the ball, but the Wanderers replied by going two up with Hunt involved in the build up.

He moved in from the right to play the ball to Westwood who had time to pick his spot, sending a right-foot shot into the roof of the net.

Bolton had scored this goal with only ten men after Anderson had been assisted off the park, getting injured in a challenge with Finch.

The visitors made some promising moves but an understrength Bolton side were worthy leaders at the interval with Hunt receiving a standing ovation.

The new forward continued to cause problems for Albion, his constructive touch forcing Finch into a late challenge which the referee took exception to by taking his name.

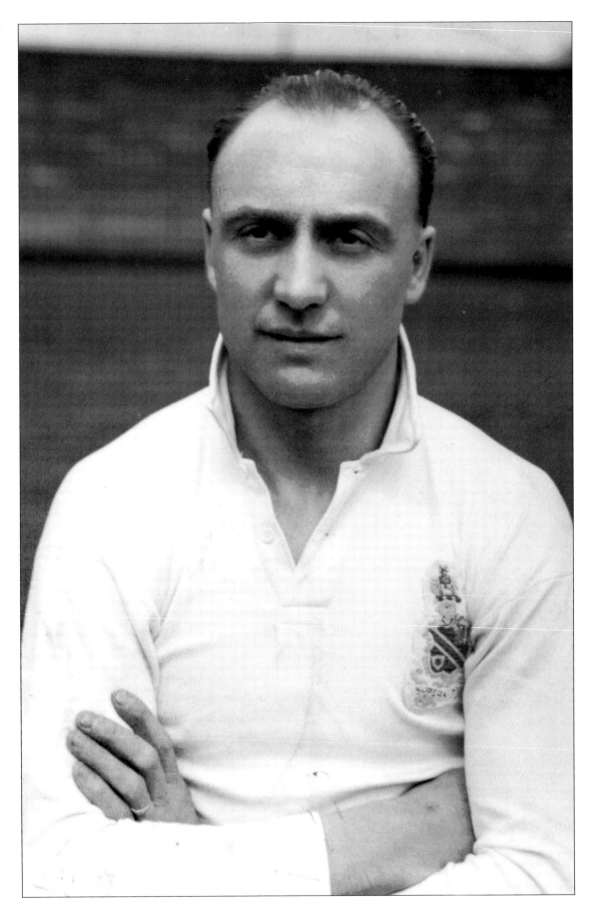

Bolton went three up after 70 minutes but at some cost. George Taylor set up Westwood and, as he shot the goal, he was severely kicked on the left shin. After treatment on the touch-line he had to be carried to the dressing-room leaving his side down to nine men.

Despite this further handicap the visitors never really threatened and Bolton were worthy winners.

Bolton Wanderers: Hanson; Tennant, Hubbick, Goslin, Atkinson, Taylor, Jones, Grosvenor, Hunt, Westwood, Anderson.
West Bromwich Albion: Adams; Finch, C.E.Shaw, Lowery, Sandford, Rix, Mahon, Heaselgrave, Richardson, Clarke, Johnson.

Attendance: 23,098
Referee: H.T.McBride (Crewe)

Albert Geldard, signed for Bolton from Everton but the outbreak of war ruined his career with Wanderers.

Trotters Win Last Game Before War
2 September 1939
BOLTON WANDERERS 2 PORTSMOUTH 1

Having lost narrowly at Chelsea and won at Stoke in their opening First Division fixtures, the Wanderers made their bow at Burnden with the visit of Cup holders Portsmouth.

It was, however, a game played in an atmosphere of foreboding, with many believing it would be the last played in Bolton under the present League system for some time due to the imminent war situation.

Portsmouth scored an early gift goal. Goslin, attempting to play his way out of trouble, got caught in possession and Barlow nipped in to put his side ahead.

This came as a shock to the Wanderers, who were finding Portsmouth's offside trap hard to beat, but an equaliser came by virtue of a mistake after 13 minutes.

From a throw-in on the right Harry Hubbick gained possession and lobbed the ball 40 yards towards the visitors' goal. Goalkeeper Walker came out to collect it on the bounce but Hunt's presence worried him and the ball passed over his head into the net.

Six minutes from the interval Don Howe put Bolton ahead with a left-foot shot. Wharton had tried to cover Howe but the Wanderer persisted, beating the half-back to get in his effort.

Although clearly deserving the points, Bolton almost threw them away in a decline late in the game. Twice Hunt erred in not slipping passes to Westwood to make sure whilst Worrall twice went close for Portsmouth.

The following morning war was declared and the League came to a close when the Management Committee met to officially suspend activities and announce that contracts between clubs and players would be automatically terminated.

The next game at Burnden Park was a fortnight later when Manchester United visited for a friendly. The Bolton

side was selected from members of staff in the Bolton Artillery and gas masks were in evidence everywhere amongst the crowd of 4,830.

Bolton Wanderers: Hanson; Winter, Hubbick, Goslin, Hurst, Taylor, Geldard,

Howe, Hunt, Westwood, Rothwell.
Portsmouth: Walker; Morgan, Rochford, Smith, Rowe, Wharton, Worrall, McAlinden, Anderson, Barlow, Parker.

Attendance: 12,992
Referee: P.Stevens (Luton)

The War Brings Football to an End
18 May 1940
BOLTON WANDERERS 4 ACCRINGTON STANLEY 1

The first season of wartime football, in the North-West Division of the War Regional League, closed at Burnden Park with a visit from Accrington.

The Wanderers had made a good ending to the term, with only one loss and five victories in the last half dozen games, but the smallest crowd, only 500, were on the terraces.

The only change to the Bolton side that had won 8-1 five days previously at Southport was the inclusion of Whalley for Connor at left-half.

Both sides missed a couple of easy chances in as many minutes, Jones creating the first for Bolton by taking Hunt's pass to the near post before

rolling it to Sidebottom who failed with an open goal before him.

The next Bolton advance brought the opening goal. Hunt had the ball at his feet in the penalty area when Ash tripped him. Hunt got up to score from the spot after four minutes play.

Play became tame, the Wanderers spoiling their approach work by slowness in front of goal. The crowd began to cheer Accrington's livelier efforts and welcomed a 35th-minute equaliser by Jones.

Hunt immediately restored the Wanderers lead by dashing past Ash and Johnson and beating Robinson as he came out.

Chadwick and Sidebottom provided the majority of the entertainment after the interval, the little winger creating a chance that Sidebottom couldn't miss in the 57th minute.

Sidebottom made sure of the points with a fourth goal to send the small crowd home happy.

At the end of the season it wasn't certain that the Wanderers would take part in any competition that was organised for the following term. A loss had been incurred on every home match and it was increasingly difficult to find a team.

It was decided that the club would not play again during 1940 despite the offer of a number of friendly fixtures.

Bolton Wanderers: Goodall; Eastwood, Hubbick, Graham, Atkinson, Whalley, W.Jones, Cunliffe, Hunt, Sidebottom, Chadwick.
Accrington Stanley: Robinson; Johnson, Reeday, Ward, Ash, Webster, Mortimer, Dyson, Jones, Ainsworth, Seddon.

Attendance: 500
Referee: R.Duerden (Burnley)

Full-back Harry Hubbick and goalkeeper Ted Goodall continued to play football in between working down the mines.

Lofthouse Makes His Bow

22 March 1941
BOLTON WANDERERS 5 BURY 1

A surprise change was made for the return Football League North match with Bury at Burnden Park, the Wanderers looking to gain revenge for a 4-1 defeat a week earlier.

Nat Lofthouse led the Bolton attack.

Not yet 16, he had been playing well for Bacup and to accommodate him George Hunt appeared in the unusual role of right-half.

Two other amateurs also made their debuts, 'keeper Walter Grimsditch of Farnsworth St Thomas's and Harry Cload, a 17-year-old from Halliwell St Thomas's.

Bury changed their 'keeper for their fourth successive game, their debutant being William Burnham of Radcliffe Technical School.

Hunt was conspicuous with some clever manoeuvring and passing and he started the move which led to Johnson opening the score after ten minutes.

Then came a second goal with a real Sunday School League effort. It was a clearance by Banks which sent Lofthouse on the right to centre for Cload. The ball then travelled past two defenders, who stood watching, as the outside-left took his shot first time to plant the ball into the corner of the net.

Hunt was then brought down 30 yards from goal and from the free-kick Connor drove the ball past Burnham.

Davies then hit the post with a penalty for Bury, awarded after he had been brought down by Hubbick, but the visitors pulled one back through Livingstone.

After the break Lofthouse missed a couple of chances from crosses by Finan, whilst the Bury forwards were unable to sustain any attacks.

Late in the game Lofthouse capped a workmanlike debut by scoring the Wanderers' fourth and fifth goals.

The young centre-forward kept his place in the side for the remainder of the season, finishing up with 11 goals from as many games.

Bolton Wanderers: Grimsditch; Banks, Hubbick, Hunt, Atkinson, Connor, Finan, Sidebottom, Lofthouse, Johnson, Cload.
Bury: Burnham; Gorman, Hart, Jones, Watson, Griffiths, Slack, Livingstone, Davies, Dougal, Carter.

Attendance: 1,587
Referee: R.A.Mortimer (Huddersfield)

Opposite page: Nat Lofthouse, later to become an England international, began his legendary career with two goals in a 5-1 win over Bury at Burnden.

War Cup Comes to Burnden

19 May 1945
BOLTON WANDERERS 1
MANCHESTER UNITED 0

Bolton's Cup pedigree again came to the fore towards the end of the war as the large crowds returned to football.

Having accounted for Blackpool, Newcastle and Wolves, each over two legs, in the qualifying rounds of the Football League War Cup, they now faced local rivals Manchester United in the two-legged Northern Final that was to be witnessed by almost 100,000 spectators overall.

The gates were open three hours before the start to see Nat Lofthouse return after injury to lead the attack with Willie Moir stepping down.

Wanderers found progress difficult with their first move being on the left, Barrass receiving a pass from Butler that he

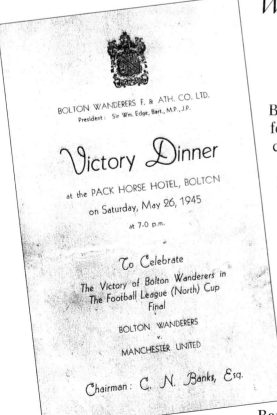

Cover of the menu for the victory dinner after Bolton defeated Manchester United in the two-legged Final.

Prisoners-of-war clear Burnden of storage baskets prior to the first leg of the Football League (North) War Cup Final against Manchester United.

volleyed towards goal only to see it blocked by Whalley.

Creating chances proved difficult due to the strong wind and, although both teams battled hard, the first half ended scoreless.

The Bolton goal had a narrow escape early after the restart. Sloan had a clear opportunity but he delayed his drive a fraction and Chadwick somehow got in the way of his colleague's hard drive.

The Wanderers were not long in changing the attack and from Woodward's pass Hunt ran through to win a corner. Woodward placed the ball so well that 'keeper Crompton had scarcely gathered it, close to the far post, when Lofthouse bundled both player and ball into the net to put Bolton ahead after 50 minutes.

This goal was enough to settle the first leg, the nearest either side coming to finding the net again begin when

Hamlett shot a 40-yard free-kick inches over the bar.

A week later Bolton received the Cup when they drew 2-2 with United at Maine Road, Malcolm Barrass equalising for the Wanderers in the final minute.

The season was completed with a 2-1 win over Chelsea at Stamford Bridge before 45,000 spectators in the Football League War Cup, North v South Final.

Bolton Wanderers: Fielding; Threlfall, Hubbick, Taylor, Hamlett, Murphy, Woodward, Hunt, Lofthouse, Barrass, Butler.
Manchester United: Crompton; Walton, Roughton, Warner, Whalley, Chilton, Chadwick, White, Bryant, Sloan, Wrigglesworth.

Attendance: 40,785
Referee: T.Smith (Atherstone)

Burnden Park's Darkest Hour

9 March 1946

The Wanderers had produced some sparkling football after the end of World War Two, especially in the FA Cup, which during 1945-46 was played over two legs.

Having beaten Blackburn Rovers, Liverpool and Middlesbrough, the Wanderers found themselves in the sixth round against Stoke City. The first leg took place at the Victoria Ground where two Ray Westwood goals made Bolton favourites to reach the semi-finals. There had been a crowd of 50,735 at Stoke and a similar attendance at Burnden was expected for the second leg on 9 March 1946.

The excitement in the town was intense, especially when it was announced that Stanley Matthews would be playing for Stoke.

The crowds began to assemble before one o'clock with the embankment filling quickly. By 2.35pm, the Railway Embankment was full, yet spectators were still getting in and thousands more were outside.

It became impossible for those entering the ground to pass along the terraces and the police decided it was time to close the turnstiles. Unfortunately the head checker couldn't be found and, during this delay, a number of people decided they wanted to leave the ground because they couldn't reach the terraces to see the game.

Twenty minutes before the kick-off the police began to help spectators out of the north-west corner on to the perimeter track. One man was trampled as an invasion began over the railway line fence on the Burnden side. The police were helpless to do anything, as the men on that side of the ground were guarding stockpiles of food stored under the Burnden stand.

The head checker was finally found and the turnstiles were shut but this

The dreadful scene at Burnden immediately after crowd safety barriers had collapsed.

didn't deter many who simply climbed over the wall or attempted to force open the doors to the turnstiles.

Ten minutes before the kick-off, a young boy found the crush too great, his father picking the padlock of the gate next to the boys' entrance to get out. Outside, a large number of people rushed in and more became trampled under foot.

A police sergeant ordered a section of the crowd to pull down the wooden perimeter fence to help relieve the crush and also to open the gates to allow people to leave. Keys or officials could not be found however and a crowd of around 1,000 climbed over a fence near to the boys' entrance.

Eventually, mounted police sealed off the area outside the ground but many simply made their way on to the railway itself.

At 2.55pm the crowd swayed as the teams came on to the field, people at the top of the terrace finding themselves forced down into the bottom corner. As the spectators pressed forward for a better view, two barriers close to the boys' entrance collapsed. People simply began to pile up on one another.

Hundreds spilled on to the track as the game kicked off and after 12 minutes play the referee was informed that there had been fatalities and he took the players from the pitch.

Thirty-three bodies were found and laid out on the pitch before being taken to mortuaries. A further 500 received first-aid, yet incredibly hardly anyone in the rest of the ground was aware of the serious nature of what had happened.

The Burnden Stand was opened for 1,000 spectators and a similar number were allowed on to the track to ease the congestion. To avoid any disorder it was decided to continue with the game and at 3.25pm play resumed and proceeded without any interval.

A scoreless draw sent Bolton into the semi-finals where they went down to Charlton Athletic at Villa Park.

The community was shocked by the magnitude of the disaster, the Mayor of Bolton opening a Relief Fund which was swelled by charity matches such as England against Scotland at Maine Road, whilst the enquiry into the disaster was well reaching.

The report of R.Moelwyn Hughes KC, appointed by the Home Secretary, Chuter Ede, found that the expectation of a 50,000 gate was reasonable. In the event, probably around 85,000 attempted to gain admittance, although the official attendance was 65,419. The disaster was unique in that no structure collapsed and it was the first inflicted by a crowd upon themselves. The Home Office Report's recommendations for alterations to the Railway Embankment were put in hand at a cost of £5,500.

Four days after the disaster, Bolton entertained Bradford in a Football League North game which attracted a crowd of only 5,162.

Today, the Normid Superstore lies on the spot of where 33 people lost their

Opposite page, top: The scene outside the Embankment prior to it being rebuilt in 1946. The white lines show where a wall was to be erected. Note the house on the site which had been used by the club since 1895. *Bottom:* Work on the new wall began after demolition of the house.

The new wall that was to be the entrance to the Embankment for almost 40 years.

lives and is commem-
orated by a plaque
unveiled in September
1992 by club president
Nat Lofthouse who played
in the game.

Just for the record, the
Bolton team that played
that day was: Hanson;
Threlfall, Hubbick, Hurst,
Hamlett, Murphy, Gel-
dard, Howe, Lofthouse,
Westwood, Woodward.

An unused
ticket for that
fateful day in
1946; and the
plaque that
can be seen on
the Normid
building at the
Embankment
end of the
ground.

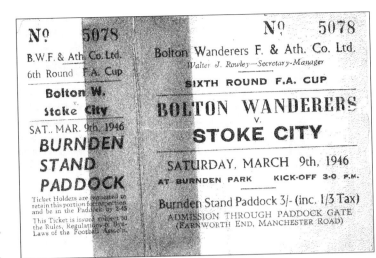

Burnden Born and Bred

JACK Nuttall had become the club's first trainer-groundsman at Pikes Lane in 1887. It was a family affair with his wife's responsibility being the team's laundry.

The move to Burnden Park in 1895 saw the Nuttalls move to the house adjacent to the ground with Jack looking after both responsibilities until 1903, when former Wolves and Everton player Jack Lewis took over the training duties. Nuttall continued to act as groundsman.

Two years after moving to Burnden in 1897, Harry (Henry) Nuttall was born in the house at Burnden and was to follow in the footsteps of his elder brother, Jimmy, in representing the club.

Jimmy had played 82 games for the Wanderers during the World War One whilst Harry began his football with St Mark's in the Bolton League before going to

Fleetwood. In December 1920, Harry (**pictur-ed**) returned home to be signed by Bolton Wanderers.

He made his League debut in September 1921 in a 1-0 home win over FA Cup holders Tottenham Hotspur. He fin-

ally settled into the half-back position, going on to make 326 first-team appearances and winning three FA Cup winners medals with the club in 1923, 1926 and 1929. He won the first of three England caps in October

1927, against Ireland in Belfast, and would possibly have won more but for the Wanderers' Cup commitments.

He left the Wanderers in May 1932 to join Rochdale and later became coach at Nelson but he wasn't away from Burnden Park long. He returned 'home' in 1935 to become second-team trainer and he remained at Burnden until his retirement in 1964. He continued to be a familiar face around the ground, taking on the duties of kit man until his death in 1969. Here, Jack Nuttall tends to the boys' entrance after the Burnden disaster in 1946.

Late Goal Seals First Home Win After the War

7 September 1946

BOLTON WANDERERS 1 PORTSMOUTH 0

The fixture list from the 1939-40 season was kept intact for use after the war and the Wanderers made history repeat itself by taking four points from their opening three First Division games.

After an opening day defeat at Chelsea and a win at Stoke, Portsmouth were the first visitors to Burnden. They had three players in the side that had played in the last League game before war was declared, whilst Bolton fielded five.

The Wanderers had the opportunity to open the scoring in the 27th minute when they were awarded a penalty after Lofthouse was brought down by Flewin.

Unfortunately Lol Hamlett drove his kick straight at Walker and he saved easily.

During the second half Froggatt hit

Bolton Wanderers team in 1946-47, the first season of post-war League football. Back row (left to right): J.Gillies, L.Hamlett, S.Hanson, W.Ridding (trainer), H.Hubbick, E.Forrest. Front row: T.Woodward, D.Howe, J.Atkinson, N.Lofthouse, R.Westwood, E.Rothwell.

the post for Pompey but the match was marked by dramatic incidents in the final five minutes.

Wanderers' 'keeper, Hanson, brought down Froggatt and the referee had no hesitation in awarding the visitors a penalty. In response to appeals from Bolton he consulted a linesman and promptly reversed his decision.

Portsmouth's players resented the referee's handling of the situation and their disappointment heightened through the fact that Bolton snatched victory seconds later with a goal by Billy Moir.

Several visiting players seemed disinclined to resume the game after the goal and when play ended three of

them had to be dragged away from the linesman who had been consulted by the referee in the penalty incident.

The Burnden crowd of 33,597 compared favourably to the attendance of 12,992 that had seen the final game between the clubs just before the hostilities.

Bolton Wanderers: Hanson; Threlfall, Hubbick, Howe, Hamlett, Forrest, Woodward, Moir, Lofthouse, Westwood, Rothwell.
Portsmouth: Walker; Rookies, Ferrier, Dickenson, Flewin, Wharton, Nutley, Reid, Froggatt, McAlinden, Parker.
Attendance: 33,597
Referee: S.Clark (London)

City Keep up Burnden FA Cup Hoodoo

25 January 1947
BOLTON WANDERERS 3 MANCHESTER CITY 3

Confidence had risen in the Bolton camp due to a run of seven League games without a win having come to an end the previous Saturday. A 3-0 win at Liverpool followed hard on the heels of a 5-1 FA Cup third-round success over Stockport at Burnden.

Bolton's reward for defeating Stockport was a local derby in the fourth round with Second Division Manchester City and an opportunity for avenging Burnden Cup exits of 1933 and 1937.

The Wanderers set off towards the Great Lever goal to make a sensational start by scoring the first goal in 30

The BOLTON WANDERERS
Football & Athletic Co. Ltd.

TEL. 900

President : SIR WILLIAM EDGE, Bart.
Directors   C. N. Banks (Chairman)   Dr. A. Cochrane   P. Duxbury   E. Prestwich, J.P
Ald. J. Entwistle, J.P.   W. Hayward   E. Gerrard   H. Warburton
WALTER J. ROWLEY, Secretary-Manager   H. ABBOTTS, Assistant-Secretary

2d.   OFFICIAL PROGRAMME   2d.

F.A. CUP—(4th Round)

BOLTON WANDERERS

VERSUS

MANCHESTER CITY

At Burnden Park, Bolton

Saturday, Jan. 25th, 1947

Kick-Off 2-45 p.m.

NEXT HOME MATCH

CENTRAL LEAGUE.   SATURDAY, FEBRUARY 1st.   Kick-Off 3.0 p.m.

WANDERERS RES. v. WEST BROMWICH A. RES.

Cover of the programme for the FA Cup-tie against Manchester City and Malcolm Barrass – hit a late equaliser for Wanderers to earn a replay.

seconds without a City player touching the ball.

Lofthouse, receiving the ball from Moir, worked the ball to Woodward who made a quick centre. Wrigglesworth gathered it inside the penalty area to leave Swift helpless with a right-foot shot into the corner of the net.

City were shook by a second goal after nine minutes, Lofthouse rising to head home a left-wing cross from Hubbick.

Bolton continued to hold the upper hand but the visitors got back into the game when a shot from Smith was only half cleared and Black found the net, this coming after 55 minutes.

Then, eight minutes later, City levelled when Black scored again from close range.

In a dramatic turnaround City made

it three goals in 12 minutes. Hanson's poor clearance fell to Capel whose low drive flew into the net off Hamlett's body.

The Wanderers saved the day with ten minutes remaining. Barrass tapped the ball over the line to make it 3-3 after a shot from Woodward had struck the inside of the far post.

Four days later City won the replay 1-0 whilst the next League game at Burnden, against Leeds United, attracted a crowd of only 4,280.

Bolton Wanderers: Hanson; Banks, Hubbick, Gillies, Hamlett, Forrest, Woodward, Moir, Lofthouse, Barrass, Wrigglesworth.
Manchester City: Swift; Williams, Barkas, Fagan, McDowall, Emptage, Dunkley, Smith, Black, Capel, Westwood.

Attendance: 41,286
Referee: G.Reader (Southampton)

Willie Moir Heads Goalscorers

7 May 1949
BOLTON WANDERERS 1 EVERTON 0

The Wanderers gave a display more on the arts and crafts by way of a finale to

another season at Burnden and, in winning this First Division match by a

Willie Moir – hit the winner against Everton to take his season's tally of goals to 25.

Opposite page, top: Don Howe leads out the Wanderers during 1948 whilst an injured Nat Lofthouse looks on from the bench.

Opposite page, bottom: Bolton Wanderers in 1948-49. Back row (left to right): W.Ridding (trainer), D.Howe, J.Roberts, S.Hanson, R.Banks, M.Barrass, D.Murphy. Front row: T.Woodward, W.Moir, N.Lofthouse, W.Rowley (manager), J.Bradley, H.McShane, M.Gillies.

relegation was never an issue, it was an ideal way of ending the season. There was an exhibition quality about the standard of play with Hernon revelling in the opportunity for some neat and close footwork in which Murphy rather surprisingly joined. Their triangular movements with McShane provided a couple of fleeting openings for Lofthouse but both efforts were blocked.

The only goal came in the 21st minute. From Woodward's free-kick near to the corner-flag, Moir leapt high to beat Sagar with a bullet header so powerful that the ball had come back into play before some of the defenders realised it had been in the net.

Everton had their opportunities to get back into the game, the best being just before half-time. The Wanderers' defence were dazzled by a slick move that created an opening for a fierce volley by Eglington producing a magnificent one-handed save by Elvy who also denied Jones from a furious free-kick. For Willie Moir it was his 25th goal of the season, all of which came in League games, and he was the only ever-present during 1948-49. His goal tally was enough to give him the honour for being the First Division's leading goalgetter.

Bolton Wanderers: Elvy; Roberts, Banks, Howe, Barrass, Murphy, Woodward, Moir, Lofthouse, Hernon, McShane.
Everton: Sagar; Saunders, Dugdale, Farrell, Jones, Lello, Powell, Wainwright, McIntosh, Stevenson, Eglington.

single goal, got less than their deserts.

It was only the club's third League win since Christmas and although

Attendance: 22,725
Referee: J.H.Parker (Macclesfield)

Cup Exit at the Hands of the Peacocks
1 February 1950
BOLTON WANDERERS 2 LEEDS UNITED 3 (AFTER EXTRA-TIME)

The referee passed Burnden Park playable for this FA Cup fourth-round replay at 11 o'clock after pacing its sandy surface from end to end. He had

no hesitation, although no one could pretend conditions were nothing but bad after a further freezing the previous night. Further rain at midday made the

The Wanderers in action against Blackpool at Burnden in April 1950.

The club's first electronic crowd counting machine being operated by secretary-manager Walter Rowley in 1950.

pitch look like a beach after a receding tide.

Four days earlier the sides had drawn 1-1 at Elland Road and the Wanderers fell behind after only three minutes in the replay. Goalkeeper Stan Hanson misjudged the flight of the ball which sailed over his head as he advanced to the near post in an attempt to collect a cross from Williams. Instead it fell to Dudley who headed home.

It was impossible to be sure what would happen to the ball in the middle of the park due to the patches of water. By half-time Leeds still held the lead but could have been three up despite being outplayed.

Four minutes after the interval the Yorkshire side went two up when Browning headed in after an attempted

clearance by Gillies had got stuck in the mud. A fast, low shot by McShane got Bolton back into the game in the 55th minute and the recovery was completed with 18 minutes left when Lofthouse equalised from a corner-kick.

Both sides went all out for the winner but it needed extra-time to decide the issue. Five minutes into the first period Leeds got what turned out to be the winner, Dudley driving into the net at close range for Leeds to progress to the fifth round and face Cardiff City.

Bolton Wanderers: Hanson; Roberts, Banks, Barrass, Gillies, Howe, McShane, Moir, Lofthouse, Bradley, Langton.
Leeds United: Searson, Dunn, Milburn, McCabe, Charles, Burden, Cochrane, Iggleden, Browning, Dudley, Williams.

Attendance; 29,440
Referee: E.Plinston (Warrington)

Big crowd on the Embankment during a match in 1950.

Coach George Hunt with Tom Woodward, Willie Moir, John Bradley, Nat Lofthouse and Harry McShane.

Bobby Langton converts a penalty on the opening day of the 1951-52 season, when Aston Villa were beaten 5-2 at Burnden. Two weeks later Manchester United were beaten as the Wanderers kept up their marvellous start to the campaign.

Doug Lishman strikes the post for Arsenal during Bolton's 3-0 win before 43,484 at Burnden in December 1950.

Trotters Defeat Red Devils to go Top

1 September 1951

BOLTON WANDERERS 1 MANCHESTER UNITED 0

Another victory kept Bolton's unbeaten start to the season intact and, hard gained though it was, it kept the Wanderers on top of the First Division. For United, it was their first defeat of the season.

An opportunist goal by Lofthouse, after he had been played onside by an opponent, decided a struggle that could easily have gone either way if Rowley had not blazed away two grand openings.

Both attacks were in the grip of strong spoiling defences and it was not often that either goal was exposed. It was a defenders' day with Chilton and Barrass unyielding stumbling blocks in the middle and Higgins challenging Redman as the best back of the day. United's debutant John Berry, transferred from Birmingham the day before the game, did well on the right wing in the Cup-tie atmosphere.

The winning goal came in the 50th minute. Codd took a right-wing corner and Moir headed goalwards. The ball came back to Moir who chipped it over defenders' heads to Lofthouse who helped it into the net as Allen rushed out.

United's players were convinced that Lofthouse was offside and they made vigorous attempts to talk the referee into consulting a linesman. They failed, as the linesman had already pointed his flag to signal a goal, the cross by Moir having taken a deflection off a United player.

The Burnden crowd of 55,477 set a new post-war League record for the ground and was the first over 50,000 since the disaster game with Stoke in 1946.

Bolton Wanderers: Hanson; Ball, Higgins, Wheeler, Barrass, Edwards, Codd, Moir, Lofthouse, Webster, Langton.
Manchester United: Allen; Carey, Redman, Gibson, Chilton, Cockburn, Berry, Pearson, Rowley, Downie, Bond.
Attendance: 55,477
Referee: E.R.S.Hill (Chester)

Ten-goal Christmas Day Thriller
25 December 1952
BOLTON WANDERERS 4 ARSENAL 6

If goals make soccer the magnet then the Christmas Day crowd at Burnden for this First Division match saw the game at its best. Inside a minute, Moir lost a great scoring chance and then put the Wanderers ahead, both being clinical moves.

Sparkling attacking play had Arsenal penned in their own half but, in characteristic Gunners fashion, they turned defence into attack when they drew level in the 12th minute, Milton dribbling around two defenders.

Webster shot against the upright for Bolton and Moir saw a header beat Kelsey but curl away from an empty net. A powerful drive from Holton hit the net and gave the Londoners a half-time lead.

Two goals in five minutes after the break, from Roper and Logie, emphasised the Gunners' mastery of

the goalmaking art and for a time they demonstrated a clear superiority of the game. Many a side would have buckled at this stage but not Bolton.

With the second half ten minutes old, Lofthouse banged in a second goal and although Arsenal promptly added two more, through a penalty kick from Daniel and a shot from Holton, the Wanderers' attack battled back with such spirit.

The margin was again reduced to two by goals from Lofthouse and Moir in the 78th and 80th minutes. The game was more alive than ever with the crowd revelling in Bolton's attacking qualities. Five minutes from time Langton won a penalty-kick. This was a great moment, a fifth now would mean there was still a chance to save the day. Unfortunately Langton's kick from the spot wasn't far enough away from

Bolton Wanderers in 1952-53. Back row (left to right): E.Bell, B.Sproston (trainer), J.Wheeler, J.Ball, S.Hanson, M.Barrass, B.Edwards, R.Codd, G.Taylor (head trainer). Front row: D.Holden, W.Moir, N.Lofthouse, W.Ridding (manager), H.Hassall, R.Langton, G.Higgins.

Right: Bobby Langton, missed a late penalty in the ten-goal thriller against the Gunners.

Below: Spectators in the early 1950's were greeted with a notice-board fitted to the front of the Manchester Road stand to advise them as to the situation in each part of the ground.

Bottom, left: Groundstaff clear the pitch for a third-round FA Cup-tie against Fulham in January 1953. Unfortunately the game was still called off when fog came down.

Bottom, right: Reseeding of the pitch takes place at Burnden Park in 1953.

Kelsey and the goalkeeper pushed the ball away to safety.

Although he had to keep out a great shot from Lofthouse in the closing moments, Kelsey had really settled the issue with his penalty save.

Bolton Wanderers: Hanson; Ball, Higgins, Wheeler, Barrass, Neill, Holden, Moir, Lofthouse, Webster, Langton.

Arsenal: Kelsey; Wade, Smith, Shaw, Daniel, Mercer, Milton, Logie, Holton, Lishman, Roper.

Attendance: 45,432
Referee: T.W.Glendenning (Sunderland)

Pompey Hit for Six
7 November 1953
BOLTON WANDERERS 6 PORTSMOUTH 1

1953 and Cup Final applications swamp Burnden Park. Bill Ridding oversees things with former players George Hunt (left) and Don Howe (right) helping out.

Portsmouth were the eighth team to try to attempt to lower the Wanderers' standard at Burnden Park during 1953-54 as six victories and one draw on home soil had placed the side in the top six of the First Division.

The south coast side had caused problems for Bolton in the recent past, having won 3-0 and 5-0 at Burnden in the previous two seasons. However, it took only five minutes for the Wanderers to break the visitors' defence. Nat Lofthouse latched on to a clearance from Stan Hanson and ran half the length of the pitch to send a low shot past Platt.

The Wanderers continued to be persistent and ten minutes later Harold Hassall made it 2-0 with an identical move to the one that brought about the opener.

Portsmouth got themselves back into the game when Harris converted a penalty after Ball had brought Dale to his knees. No sooner had this happened then play went to the other end where Gunter fouled Hassall in the penalty area and he got up to put the ball away to give the Wanderers a comfortable half-time advantage.

The referee missed a deliberate handling offence, which should have won Bolton another penalty seconds after the interval, but it took only five minutes for Hassall to complete his hat-trick when he volleyed home a Lofthouse cross.

There were ten minutes remaining when Doug Holden made a brilliant run, eluding three tackles, crowning it with a perfectly placed shot for his first goal of the season and his first from the wing position for the club.

The half-dozen was brought up when

Doug Holden,
who scored
Wanderers'
fifth goal
against
Pompey.

Ray Parry got the better of Gunter to get to the dead-ball line and cross for Lofthouse to side foot into the net.

Portsmouth were to make a second visit to Burnden that season for a fifth-round FA Cup-tie that ended scoreless although the Wanderers went on to win the replay on the south coast.

Bolton Wanderers: Hanson; Ball, T.Banks, Neill, Barrass, Bell, Holden, Moir, Lofthouse, Hassall, Parry.

Portsmouth: Platt; Gunter, Mansell, Pickett, Rutter, Dickenson, Harris, Gordon, Henderson, Reid, Dale.

Attendance: 22,441
Referee: A.Bond (London)

Battle of the Wanderers

5 February 1955
BOLTON WANDERERS 6 WOLVERHAMPTON WANDERERS 1

The odds were stacked against 17th-placed Bolton when First Division leaders Wolves visited Burnden. Only a single victory in 13 League games had seen Bolton plummet and changes were made to the forward line in an attempt to stop the slide. Willie Moir moved to outside-right for the first time in five years with Doug Holden switching to the left.

There was no indication of the goal deluge that was to come with the only score during the first half arriving in the 31st minute. From Bryan Edwards' long clearance Nat Lofthouse beat Billy Wright in the air, guiding his header to the feet of Ray Parry. The young inside-left didn't hesitate and cracked the ball on the half volley past Williams.

The second half was only a minute old when Bolton hit the net again with Eric Bell scoring a similar goal to the opener before Wolves pulled one back in the 50th minute, Hancock's centre being converted by Wilshaw.

Bolton, however, began to make the visitors' defence look ragged and Harry Webster ran in to convert a free-kick by

Bolton Wanderers in 1954. Back row (left to right): W.Ridding (manager), M.McIlwaine, J.Wheeler, J.Ball, S.Hanson, M.Barrass, E.Bell, N.Lofthouse, B.Sproston (trainer). Front row: R.Codd, D.Holden, W.Moir, W.Hayward (chairman), H.Hassall, G.Higgins, R.Parry.

later Lofthouse got a fifth. Wolves goalkeeper Bert Williams was hurt in the incident and had to be stretchered off with Ron Flowers taking over between the posts. Wolves had the opportunity to reduce the arrears when they won a penalty after Tommy Banks handled. Hancocks took the kick but his effort struck the crossbar and the rebound was cleared.

Bolton completed the half-dozen when Parry found the net to register his first hat-trick in senior football – Ray's brother, Jack, also finding the net on the same day for Derby against Port Vale.

Sunderland took over the leadership of the division but Wolves bounced back the following week with a 6-4 defeat of Huddersfield at Molineux. As for Bolton, they went on to win three of the next four games in what was their most successful spell of the season.

Bolton Wanderers: Hanson; Ball, Edwards, Wheeler, Barrass, Bell, Moir, Webster, Lofthouse, Parry, Holden.
Wolves: Williams; Stuart, Shorthouse, Slater, Wright, Flowers, Hancocks, Broadbent, Swinbourne, Wilshaw, Smith.

Attendance: 37,427
Referee: S.M.Rogers (Shrewsbury)

Holden. In the 70th minute Bolton struck a fourth when Parry slid the ball into the net off the far post and the crowd went wild when two minutes

Trotters put Four Past Pensioners
17 December 1955
BOLTON WANDERERS 4 CHELSEA 0

A week before this game, the Wanderers had demolished Birmingham City 6-0 at Burnden, with Nat Lofthouse hitting four of the goals. The prospect of more fun added almost 10,000 spectators to the attendance for the visit of Chelsea for this First Division match despite the proximity of Christmas, the crowd looking for another goal avalanche.

In ideal playing conditions the Londoners' rearguard showed considerable efficiency. Bolton, however, went ahead on the first occasion that

Lofthouse got a clear chance with his head. Parry was the man to make the perfect cross and he was the first to be congratulated by the scorer.

Six minutes before half-time Lofthouse netted again but the referee disallowed the goal after the centre-forward had knocked over Robertson in winning the ball.

Three minutes later Bolton did make it 2-0 when Ralph Gubbins swept Doug Holden's flag-kick into the net. Chelsea, the previous season's League champions, were looking badly outplayed and this continued into the second half.

Seven minutes after the restart Holden beat Willemse and crossed a perfect ball for Lofthouse to head the perfect goal.

The Wanderers continued to play a grand attacking game with Chelsea's only respite coming when Blunstone had a goal-bound shot kicked away by Hartle.

Lofthouse went on to complete his hat-trick with another well-worked goal, slipping past Saunders before planting the ball in the net.

The Wanderers held defensive solidarity until Barrass suffered a leg strain and went up into the forward line with Edwards reverting to centre-half. This result coupled with the win over Birmingham rekindled hopes of a championship challenge but a run of four League defeats over the Christmas and New Year holiday put paid to that.

Bolton Wanderers: Grieves; Hartle, Banks, Wheeler, Barrass, Edwards, Holden, Stevens, Lofthouse, Parry, Gubbins.
Chelsea: Tindall; Blunstone, Bentley, Brabrook, Parsons, Saunders, Wicks, Armstrong, Willemse, Sillett, Robertson.

Attendance: 24,129
Referee: B.A.Buckle (Peterborough)

The Bolton side that defeated Chelsea 4-0 at Burnden. Back row (left to right): R.Hartle, B.Edwards, K.Grieves, J.Wheeler, R.Parry, N.Lofthouse. Front row: T.Banks, D.Holden, M.Barrass, D.Stevens, R.Gubbins.

Busby Babes Beaten at Burnden
10 November 1956
BOLTON WANDERERS 2 MANCHESTER UNITED 0

The Busby Babes were given a lesson by Bolton in this First Division match before Burnden Park's best League attendance of the season. United hadn't been beaten away from home whilst the Wanderers, although unbeaten in six games, hadn't won at Burnden since 15 September.

Most of the opening ten minutes play took place in the Bolton half of the field, but then the Wanderers broke away to go ahead. Mancunian Doug Holden, who wasn't a prolific scoring marksman, got himself into the United penalty area to receive an accurate square pass and he placed a low shot inside the far post with Wood well beaten.

Up to the interval neither attack could sustain an advance for long periods due to the close marking and deadly tackling from both defences. Brilliant clearances from Byrne and Duncan Edwards cut short promising Bolton attacks whilst the crowd were bemused to see the referee penalise Higgins for a well-timed tackle on Taylor.

Bolton's second goal came when Bryan Edwards hooked the ball across for Stevens to turn it to Allcock who pushed it past Wood as he scampered off his line. This goal broke United's heart and the Wanderers began to dominate by having more method than the champions.

United managed only two more shots which failed to worry Eddie Hopkinson

These were the days of big attendances in football and Burnden was no exception, even on a midweek afternoon. Here the Great Lever End crowd gathers to cheer Bolton on to an FA Cup replay victory over Huddersfield Town in January 1956.

Right: Bryan Edwards – ever present during the season – created the Trotters' second goal against Manchester United.

who was playing in only his 17th League game for the Wanderers. The longer the game went on the more Bolton exercised their superiority and forced United into mistakes. Banks, on the other hand, brought the house down with a succession of terrific tackles to outwit United's winger Berry.

The following March the Wanderers went on to complete the double over the champions with a 2-0 success at Old Trafford.

Bolton Wanderers: Hopkinson; Hartle, Banks, Hennin, Higgins, Edwards, Holden, Stevens, Allcock, Parry, Gubbins.
Manchester United: Wood; Foulkes, Byrne, Colman, Jones, Edwards, Berry, Whelan, Taylor, Charlton, Pegg.

Attendance: 39,922
Referee: E.S.Oxley (South Kirkby)

Wanderers Win Battle of the Roses

12 January 1957
BOLTON WANDERERS 5 LEEDS UNITED 3

The Wanderers began to dispel the Burnden Park hangover from the previous week's FA Cup defeat at the hands of Blackpool. After only four minutes play in this First Division game, Harry Webster set up Ralph Gubbins who cut in to send a right-foot shot past Wood in the Leeds goal.

On the quarter hour Leeds equalised when Charles burst through the middle unchallenged and sent a clever shot past Hopkinson. Four minutes later the Yorkshire side went ahead, Charles heading home a free-kick taken by Meek.

Their lead, however, lasted only three minutes, Lofthouse feinting past Marsden to get a clear run to drive home the equaliser. Bolton then caught Leeds unawares and an angled drive by Lofthouse from six yards whistled past Wood before he could react.

Five goals in the opening 23 minutes had left the crowd breathless and they had to wait until a minute before half-time to see Bolton increase their lead. From a cross by Stevens, Lofthouse Dunn and Marsden all threw themselves at the ball and it went into the net off full-back Dunn.

The second half developed into a brawl, Gubbins and Gibson were booked and the niggling fouls prevented flowing football. Full-blooded tackling from both sides showed that tempers had become frayed.

Leeds reduced the arrears in the 78th minute, Meek's drive hitting the net after Hopkinson had failed to hold on to an attempted cross with Charles in attendance.

Five minutes from full-time the Trotters secured the points with their fifth goal. Lofthouse crossed from the right and he found Gubbins who set up Holden to hit a first-time shot from 20 yards into the roof of the net. After the game the Wanderers found themselves in sixth spot whilst Leeds were seventh.

Bolton Wanderers: Hopkinson; Hartle, Threlfall, Hennin, Higgins, Edwards, Holden, Stevens, Lofthouse, Webster, Gubbins.

Leeds United: Wood; Dunn, Hair, Gibson, Marsden, Kerfoot, Meek, Charles, Brook, Crowe, Overfield.

Attendance: 25,705
Referee: R.Wood (Sunderland)

A Bolton side in the early part of the 1956-57 season. Back row (left to right): J.Ball, B.Edwards, J.Higgins, E.Hopkinson, D.Hennin, R.Hartle. Front row: D.Holden, D.Stevens, N.Lofthouse, R.Parry, R.Gubbins.

A New Era at Burnden Park

At a cost of £25,000, the erection of floodlighting at Burnden Park brought about a new era for the ground. Installation began in May 1957 after approval had been sought from the local authorities, Town and Country Planning, Police and British Transport Authorities.

Robert Watson & Co (Constructional Engineers) Ltd, designed, fabricated, and erected the towers. The new Bolton landmarks, 160 feet tall, became a part of the town's skyline. Each pylon, four in each corner of the ground, were anchored with eight bolts one and three quarter inches in diameter and taller than the average man. The 160 feet pylons were made up of 150 feet of steel and 10 feet of foundations which were laid by Bolton and Hayes Ltd.

The galvanised steel was delivered to the ground by mid-June 1957 and fixing was completed by the end of August. The lighting experts then got to work to install the 48 x 1500 watt lights on each tower. Each light was fitted with either a plain or rippled mirror depending upon the position and the area that needed illuminating.

Not only was the electrical work for the floodlights completed but also the 170 lighting points around the ground. Exit areas, pay boxes, the stands and

In the late 1950s Burnden's new floodlights tower over the ground during a visit from Tottenham Hotspur.

February 1987 and Burnden's new floodlight pylons are set to replace the original ones built in 1957.

the car-park were all covered along with a standby battery back up in case of power failure. The total floodlight load was 288 kilowatts whilst the emergency lighting totalled 15 kilowatts.

It was claimed that the total wattage from the GEC floodlights and Osram Lamps on the towers would be sufficient to provide first-class street lighting all the way from Burnden Park to Bloomfield Road, home of Blackpool Football Club.

On Monday, 14 October 1957, unbeaten Scottish First Division leaders Hearts were the first club to play the Wanderers underneath the new lights which were switched on by the chairman Mr H.Warburton. A crowd of 21,058 saw a 1-1 draw with Terry Allcock getting the Trotters' goal.

A floodlit friendly against Blackburn Rovers a fortnight later had to be postponed but on 4 November 1957 the Wanderers entertained Russian Army team CDSA Moscow under the lights. A crowd of 34,139, which was bettered only once in League games at Burnden that season, saw Bolton score three early goals and eventually win 3-1.

Nat Lofthouse, who had to leave the field injured, a Ray Parry penalty, and Nat's replacement Ralph Gubbins were the goalgetters. The first competitive game under the lights was an FA Youth Cup second-round tie which saw the Wanderers defeat Huddersfield Town 3-2.

Gone were the days of 2-15pm Saturday afternoon kick-offs in the middle of winter and evening games moved to the later traditional 7-30pm starting time.

The first real change to the lighting system came in September 1975 when more powerful lights were installed. These were officially switched on by county councillor Walter Walsh prior to a 3-1 League Cup second-round defeat by Coventry City.

In February 1987 two new slimline pylons were built on the Embankment End when the Co-operative development commenced. The old towers were used for the last time for a Freight Rover Trophy game against Chester City. The visitors won 2-1 with Steve Thompson missing a penalty two minutes from time for Bolton.

The new pylons were in use for the first time on 25 February 1987 for a Central League game against Huddersfield Town. Over the next few months the old towers were dismantled and in the close season two new pylons were erected on the Great Lever side.

Let There Be Light
14 October 1957
BOLTON WANDERERS 1 HEART OF MIDLOTHIAN 1

The £25,000 investment in floodlights at Burnden Park was celebrated with the visit of Scottish club Heart of Midlothian who, by coincidence, had switched on their own lights at Tynecastle Park the previous week against Hibernian.

The Wanderers had been the first-ever visitors to Tynecastle Park in April 1886 and Hearts had been regular visitors to Bolton in pre-League days. The lights were switched on by the Wanderers' chairman, Mr H.Warbur-ton, but the weather almost disrupted the proceedings. The heavy mist which hung over the ground was exactly what was not wanted and, whilst it was obvious that the lights would be first class under normal conditions, visibility was not up to the desired standard.

None of the 21,058 spectators had a clear view of the entertaining game, both teams playing as if it was a challenge match between England and Scotland, the visitors making it obvious why they were unbeaten in the Scottish League Division One.

The Wanderers had their chances, especially one which fell to Deakin in the first half, and they put in a storming finish, but on the night's play Hearts were the superiors in control and use of the ball.

Both goals had narrow escapes before Wardhaugh put Hearts ahead in the 53rd minute with a lovely gliding header from Blackwood's cross, the ball going in off the foot of an upright.

Twelve minutes from the end Allcock equalised with a penalty-kick and, although it became difficult to follow the play due to the fog, the visitors' goal appeared to have several close calls immediately afterwards. In the gloom a shot from Edwards struck the woodwork whilst 17-year-old goalkeeper Marshall made some good saves. One of the stars for Hearts was young Dave Mackay.

Bolton Wanderers: Dean; Hartle, Banks, Hennin, Higgins, B.Edwards, Birch, Deakin, Lofthouse, Allcock, Holden.
Hearts: Marshall; Kirk, Thompson, Mackay, Glidden, Higgins, Young, Murray, Bauld, Wardhaugh, Blackwood.

Attendance: 21,058
Referee: J.H.Clough (Bolton)

Parry Strikes Cup Winner
1 March 1958
BOLTON WANDERERS 2 WOLVERHAMPTON WANDERERS 1

This FA Cup sixth-round tie was 90 minutes of concentrated Cup excitement that had knees shaking with the thrill of it all, that had tears of joy rolling down the cheeks of Wanderers' manager Bill Ridding and left Wolves chief Stan Cullis almost speechless.

Cullis clearly had chagrin and frustration written across his face as he saw his champions cast away the chance of a League and Cup double. He saw Wolves hit Bolton's posts and crossbar half a dozen times whilst defenders rescued goalkeeper Eddie Hopkinson. On no less than four occasions Roy Hartle saved 'Hoppy' when he was 'lost' way out of goal – Tommy Banks did likewise twice – and six shots were blotted out in as many minutes.

Bolton proved, however, that they had everything needed for FA Cup fighting. Skill, punch, toughness and superb fitness. Top triumph of the game went to Bolton inside-left Ray Parry, despite being carried off with eight minutes to go with a cut lip and concussion. When he came round in the dressing-room he could still smile after his memory was jolted back to the realisation that he had scored the winner.

It was inside-right Dennis Stevens who rounded off a perfect move to put Bolton in front – Lofthouse to Birch and over to Stevens who raced in to crash a 27th-minute goal.

Two minutes later the head of Bobby Mason flicked a Deeley cross home for Wolves and the battle was really on. Fifty-six minutes had gone when Nat Lofthouse, who had been the complete master of Billy Wright, chased a long ball from Derek Hennin down the centre. He sprawled over 'keeper Malcolm Finlayson who handled the ball outside the 18-yard line. Wolves players lined up for the free-kick.

Parry feinted as if to clip the ball across the goal but saw a gap appear in the wall and quickly floated it through into the corner of the net to leave everyone flat-footed. It was a pity that Parry, whose moment of inspiration

Nat Lofthouse leaps over Wolves' goalkeeper Malcolm Finlayson during the battle of the Wanderers.

Below: The FA Cup comes to Burnden again. Bill Ridding, Bert Sproston, George Taylor and George Hunt hold the smile.

had meant so much, was not there at the finish to receive the crowd's roar of satisfaction.

Bolton Wanderers: Hopkinson; Hartle, Banks, Hennin, Higgins, Edwards, Birch, Stevens, Lofthouse, Parry, Holden.
Wolverhampton Wanderers: Finlayson; Stuart, Harris, Clamp, Wright, Flowers, Deeley, Broadbent, Murray, Mason, Mullen.

Attendance: 56,306
Referee: A.Holland (Barnsley)

Above: The Wanderers celebrate on the Town Hall steps in May 1958. Nat Lofthouse has a sure hold on the Cup.

Left: The Wanderers chair comedian Ted Loone on a Burnden visit to see the Cup.

Lost in the Fog

15 November 1958
BOLTON WANDERERS 6 MANCHESTER UNITED 3

After the previous season's FA Cup success the Wanderers were looking to impose themselves for a challenge in the League championship. Only one defeat in the opening nine games showed that they could be considered serious contenders but subsequent home defeats by Burnley and West Ham now brought that thought into question. A rebuilt Manchester United, facing the Wanderers for the first time since the FA Cup Final, would test Bolton who were without their injured captain Nat Lofthouse.

Fog sheathed Burnden – but it did nothing to hold up a tremendous traffic in goals. Altogether there were nine of them, although much of the activity between the posts went unseen by large sections of the crowd. It was a match laden with a Cup-tie atmosphere – although the conditions were declared fit only at 2.20pm after experiments with the floodlights had only made matters worse.

United gave a League debut to Warren Bradley who had been on Bolton's books as an amateur whilst at Durham University. Bryan Edwards put the Wanderers ahead after six minutes with a low shot just inside the post and Dennis Stevens made it two when he headed home a free-kick conceded by United full-back Ian Greaves.

Alex Dawson pulled one back for United from a corner but two minutes from half-time a 30-yard shot by Stevens left Harry Gregg standing for a Bolton third. Bobby Charlton shot United's second from Wilf McGuinness' free-kick but a Ralph Gubbins header – lost in the fog – restored Wanderers' two-goal advantage.

Dawson's diving header from Bradley's cross made it 4-3 but a penalty, converted by Ray Parry, again gave Bolton a cushion. The game was becoming farcical as no one could see from one end of the pitch to the other. The scoring was completed by Ralph Gubbins although no one knew how the goal came about!

Bolton Wanderers: Hopkinson; Hartle, Banks, Hennin, Higgins, Edwards, Birch, Stevens, Gubbins, Parry, Holden.
Manchester United: Gregg, Foulkes, Greaves, Goodwin, Cope, McGuinness, Bradley, Quixall, Dawson, Charlton, Scanlon.

Attendance: 33,358
Referee: A.W.Luty (Leeds)

Dennis Stevens – two goals in the fog against Manchester United.

Late Goal Stops Trotters' Cup Progress

14 February 1959

BOLTON WANDERERS 2 PRESTON NORTH END 2

FA Cup holders, Bolton Wanderers, were drawn at home for the first time in the fifth round of the 1959 competition after having defeated both Scunthorpe United and Wolverhampton Wanderers away from home in the previous rounds. Preston had defeated Derby County, after a replay, and Bradford City, but a close encounter was expected as only a point separated the clubs in the First Division – both residing in the top seven.

The Wanderers took to the field in red whilst North End wore blue. Apart from a dangerous back pass, which Lynne gathered only just in time as Parry dashed in, Bolton were not seen much in attack during the early stages.

Things changed after 12 minutes when Milne fouled Parry 30 yards from goal. Parry placed the ball and thumped it hard, his left-foot drive finding a gap to the left of Lynne to put Bolton one up.

North End equalised two minutes after the interval when Campbell ran in from the wing to capitalise on Bolton's failure to clear the danger, but in the 75th minute the Wanderers regained the lead, Hartle and Parry combining to set up Birch who converted with a low left-foot shot.

Lofthouse struck the bar and Holden had a strong penalty appeal waved away after he had been brought down. Five minutes from time Hartle brought down Mayers in the corner of the penalty area and the referee awarded a penalty. Hopkinson saved Thompson's kick but couldn't recover it before the inside-forward ran in to put away the rebound for Preston's equaliser. In an exciting finale Lynne had to make brave saves from both Stevens and Lofthouse. Preston could be pleased with their showing for they had been disorganised by a flu epidemic. Four days later the sides again drew at Deepdale, but the tie was decided in the Wanderers favour by a Nat Lofthouse goal in the second replay at Ewood Park. The crowd at Burnden was the largest since 9 March 1946.

Bolton Wanderers: Hopkinson; Hartle, Banks, Hennin, Higgins, Edwards, Birch, Stevens, Lofthouse, Parry, Holden.

Preston North End: Lynne; Cunningham, Walton, Milne, Mattinson, Smith, Campbell, Thompson, Alston, Lambert, Mayers.

Attendance: 58,692
Referee: B.M.Griffiths (Newport)

Nat Lofthouse, scored the goal which won the Ewood second replay for the Wanderers.

Extra-time FA Cup Win Against Shakers
14 January 1960
BOLTON WANDERERS 4 BURY 2 (AFTER EXTRA-TIME)

The Wanderers side that defeated Bury in the FA Cup. Back row (left to right): D.Hennin, J.Higgins, E.Hopkinson, R.Hartle, G.Stanley, S.Farrimond. Front row: B.Birch, R.Parry, D.Stevens, F.Hill, D.Holden.

The Wanderers were having their best spell of the season in the First Division, three consecutive victories, including wins at Wolves and Everton putting them in the top six. In the third round of the FA Cup they were drawn away at local Third Division side Bury and, as the saying goes, the formbook goes out of the window in local derbies. A 1-1 draw at Gigg Lane, before the ground's record attendance, meant a return to Burnden four days later for the replay.

Bolton, playing in old gold, were guilty of making too many defensive errors and had Ray Parry to thank for a piece of individualism that changed the course of the game.

Dennis Stevens put the Wanderers ahead in the 26th minute with a close-range header from Freddie Hill's short

centre but Bury equalised seven minutes later through Brian Calder.

Within a further two minutes the Third Division side took the lead, Don Watson forcing the ball home after he had been unmarked at a corner. Bury had the opportunities to increase their lead and looked much more comfortable on the snow-covered pitch.

Looking down and out, with 15 minutes left, Parry was sent away by Doug Holden. He went past three opponents, leaving them floundering as he checked and side-stepped his way to a shooting position, rounding off by slipping the ball past Adams for the equaliser.

Thus reprieved, the Wanderers went into extra-time in greater heart and had

much the better of things. Brian Birch cut in to score with a low left-foot drive 20 minutes into extra-time and seven minutes later Parry secured a fourth-round tie at West Brom with Bolton's fourth.

Holden's brilliant run had seen him switch on a turn of speed that had taken him clear and his perfect cross found Parry who swept the ball into the net. The Wanderers had finally won the day the hard way.

Bolton Wanderers: Hopkinson; Hartle, Farrimond, Hennin, Higgins, Stanley, Birch, Hill, Stevens, Parry, Holden.
Bury: Adams; Robertson, Conroy, Turner, Bunner, Atherton, Calder, Watson, Holden, Neill, Hubbard.

Attendance: 43,616
Referee: K.Howley (Middlesbrough)

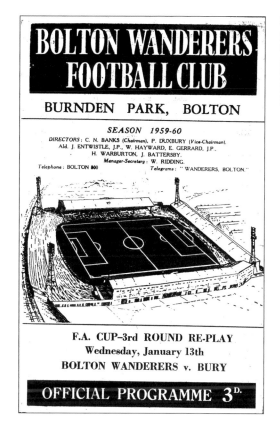

Cover of the programme for the Bury Cup game, with its familiar illustration of Burnden Park.

The Football League Cup Comes to Burnden Park
19 October 1960
BOLTON WANDERERS 5 HULL CITY 1

If for nothing else, the first Football League Cup game, a first-round replay, to be staged at Burnden will be remembered for Bill McAdams' goal, Wanderers' last of five. Receiving the ball from Freddie Hill, the Irishman slipped through the Hull defence, feinting and side-stepping each defender before drawing out the 'keeper, beating his desperate lunge and then rolling the ball into an empty net.

But this speedy entertaining match was not dependent for its success on this one McAdams masterpiece. After a goalless draw at Boothferry Park it took only four minutes for Burnden to witness its first goal in the competition. The honour fell to McAdams who put Bolton ahead with a downward header from Brian Birch's oblique cross.

On the half-hour Birch himself got on to the score-sheet and five minutes later the tie was virtually settled. From a free-kick by Birch, Hill connected on to the rebound off the wall to shoot past Bernard Fisher. Thus the Third Division side, despite some attractive midfield play, found themselves three down at the interval.

Hill netted Bolton's fourth in the 65th minute with a breathtaking cross shot but plucky Hull got some consolation five minutes later. Former Wanderer Ralph Gubbins converted Jackie Sewell's centre to register Hull's first goal in the new competition.

The evening was rounded off with McAdams wonder goal, leaving the spectators in no doubt that the League Cup was going to be much more than the FA Cup's poor relation, if this sort of game continued to be produced.

Interest in the competition continued

Above: The Wanderers in front of Burnden ready to leave on an end-of-season tour to Germany, Belgium and Spain in 1960.

Right: Billy McAdams, scorer of Wanderers' first League Cup goal.

to the fourth round for Bolton when Rotherham sprung a surprise by winning at Burnden. But that was only after a 6-2 home win over Grimsby, including a Nat Lofthouse hat-trick, and a win over Darlington that attracted a record crowd at Feethams.

Bolton Wanderers: Hopkinson; Hartle, Farrimond, Hennin, Higgins, Stanley, Holden, Stevens, McAdams, Hill, Birch.
Hull City: Fisher; Davidson, Garvey, Collinson, Feasey, Bulless, Clarke, Sewell, Chilton, Price, Gubbins.

Attendance: 10,781
Referee: N.N.Hough (Macclesfield)

E for B and Franny Lee!
5 November 1960
BOLTON WANDERERS 3 MANCHESTER CITY 1

There were fireworks galore when the Wanderers defeated Manchester City for only their fourth First Division success of the season. The game was

notable for a debut by a forward on each side. Francis Lee – a 16-year-old Westhoughton-born winger made his first senior start for the Wanderers. In sharply contrasting circumstances, Gerry Baker opened his career with City after being the subject of a big-money transfer deal during the week from St Mirren.

In a sensational opening Nat Lofthouse beat Bert Trautmann and sent a shot crashing against the upright. The Wanderers only had to wait until the 12th minute, however, before taking the lead. After Dennis Stevens had been brought down just outside the penalty area, Graham Stanley hit a free-kick that took a deflection on its way into the net.

Five minutes later, a Stevens centre evaded Lofthouse and McAdams, but Lee came bundling in head down to nod the ball into the net off the foot of the post for a debut goal.

City's Denis Law and Wanderers' centre-half John Higgins were involved in a fracas – the Scottish international getting his name taken. The visitors got back into the game in the 35th minute when Law raced in at the far post to convert a low cross from Colin Barlow,

but Bolton made the points secure with a third goal in the 65th minute. From Lee's corner Lofthouse sent a header

George Taylor passes on tips to a group of players including Francis Lee who made his debut against Manchester City.

Eddie Hopkinson saves bravely at the feet of Gerry Baker. Denis Law looks on.

rocketing into the net out of Traut-mann's reach.

This goal was to be something of a milestone as it was to be the last League goal scored by Lofthouse on Burnden Park. Despite the mud the team gave all they had in this thrilling if sometimes disorderly match. Lee – a mud splashed figure – was applauded off the field for his gutsy performance.

Bolton Wanderers: Hopkinson; Hartle, Cooper, Stanley, Higgins, Cunliffe, Lee, Lofthouse, McAdams, Stevens, Holden.

Manchester City: Trautmann; Betts, Sear, Barnes, Plenderleith, Shawcross, Barlow, Law, Hannah, Baker, Colbridge.

Attendance: 34,005
Referee: W.Clements (West Bromwich)

Trotters Trample on Tottenham
8 December 1962
BOLTON WANDERERS 1 TOTTENHAM HOTSPUR 0

Once again the Wanderers proved they could rise to the big occasion by taking the points in this First Division match against a classy Spurs side. Having lost 5-0 at Aston Villa the previous Saturday, the Wanderers bounced back in style.

The Burnden crowd were thrilled when Hill slipped past Norman and swept the ball outside to Butler. His final push towards goal was picked up by Lee and flicked towards the far corner where Brown dived to save. There was a bigger thrill soon after when Hill again made the initial move to Deakin who passed to Davies to create a clear shooting opportunity. The shot was a good one and Brown

The Wanderers line up for the camera in 1962. Back row (left to right): D.Hatton, A.Smith, E.Hopkinson, R.Hartle. Middle row: J.Threlfall, D.Holden, B.Edwards, W.Rimmer, S.Farrimond. Front row: P.Deakin, R.McGarry, W.Davies, F.Hill, B.Pilkington.

made a wonderful save at the expense of a corner.

There was a contrast in styles as Spurs moved up in close passing formation whilst the Wanderers trusted more to the long pass. Twice the referee failed to spot his linesmen flagging for infringements but he found a lot of his own of a trivial kind.

Brown had to be quick to clear a few good chances from Davies and Lee, and he was much more the busier of the two 'keepers, although before half-time Hopkinson had to save from Greaves.

Within five minutes of the restart, Spurs could have gone ahead from a choice Greaves-Jones raid. When the centre came over, Allen had only to head accurately but he put the ball over the bar.

Spurs began to dominate as the match wore on, their pressure winning them a number of corner-kicks. Hill and Lee switched positions late on and this led to a goal-getting raid with only five minutes left. Hill pushed the final pass to Deakin, who side-stepped a defender before ramming the ball into the net. It was a long-awaited goal but worth the delay.

There was to be a delay before Bolton's next League game – over two months passed by when one of the worst winters on record set in.

Bolton Wanderers: Hopkinson; Hartle, Farrimond, Stanley, Edwards, Rimmer, Lee, Hill, Davies, Deakin, Butler.
Tottenham Hotspur: Brown; Baker, Henry, Blanchflower, Norman, Mackay, Medwin, Clayton, Allen, Greaves, Jones.
Attendance: 20,737
Referee: A.W.Sparling (Grimsby)

29-year Spell in Top Flight Ends
24 April 1964
BOLTON WANDERERS 0 WOLVERHAMPTON WANDERERS 4

Scores of telegrams and telephone messages of good luck poured into Burnden Park for a game from which Bolton had to get at least a point to stay in the First Division. Written off as relegation certainties by mid-March, an unbeaten run of six games had given Bolton an escape route in this Friday evening fixture. Ipswich Town were already down – the other place would be between Bolton and Birmingham City.

The game was only two minutes old when an easy chance fell at the feet of winger Jimmy Davison. Unfortunately for Bolton he placed his shot outside the posts and that miss cost his side their one great chance of hitting the winning trail.

Wolves went ahead after 25 minutes and the writing was on the wall. Flowers unleashed a typical rocket shot which Hopkinson could only knock aside and there was Crawford on his own to tap it in.

It seemed as if Bolton may get the early goal during the opening stages of the second half. The ball fell straight to Lee's feet – the equaliser for certain – or so it appeared. But the centre-forward's first-time sweep was mistimed and Davies easily picked up the ball instead of fishing it out of the back of the net.

In the 55th minute Melia ran in for Wolves and passed to an unmarked Crawford who once again added the final touch. A minute later Le Flem crossed to Knowles on the far side who rammed home Wolves' third.

An injury to Bromley robbed Bolton of their best forward and try as they did the ten sound men couldn't make any impression. Crawford completed his hat-trick with Wolves fourth goal in the 85th minute when he converted a cross

Action from the visit of Tottenham Hotspur in December 1963. This time the Wanderers went down 3-1.

from Thomson. Thus Bolton's fate finally rested with Sheffield United's ability to avoid defeat at Birmingham the following afternoon. The Midlands side took the points which ended Bolton's 29-year spell in the First Division. The last time relegation had been suffered it needed only two seasons for a return to the top flight – times, however, had changed.

Bolton Wanderers: Hopkinson; Hartle, Farrimond, Rimmer, Edwards, Lennard, Davison, Bromley, Lee, Hatton, Taylor.

Wolverhampton Wanderers: Davies; Showell, Thomson, Flowers, Woodfield, Woodruff, Crowe, Knowles, Crawford, Melia, Le Flem.

Attendance: 27,808
Referee: W.N.Holian (Chesterfield)

Liverpool manager Bill Shankly and his Wanderers counterpart Bill Ridding have a heated discussion about the state of the Burnden pitch in February 1963. The game was called off.

The early 1960's saw further face lifts around Burnden Park. The players tunnel was concreted whilst steps were built behind the Burnden Stand to allow spectators access all the way around the ground. Standing on the slope on the extreme right is foreman Bert Gregory and next to him is a youthful Francis Lee.

Bolton supporter Roger Hunt scores against his favourites for Liverpool.

Wyn the Leap Hits Hat-trick
2 September 1964
BOLTON WANDERERS 3 SOUTHAMPTON 0

After taking only one point from their opening three Second Division games, the Wanderers finally got their promotion push on the road with a comprehensive midweek win over Southampton and Welsh centre-forward Wyn Davies filled the picture in the 3-0 win. His most dashing and effective game since he joined the club from Wrexham, brought him all three goals from accurate headers, propelled in Lofthouse style and they not only won the match, but probably guaranteed him another Welsh cap.

Wyn 'the leap' Davies – a hat-trick against The Saints.

He also produced real shots of power. The first missed the target by inches, the second from five yards tipped over by Hollowbread. After that it was his head that was to be feared when, after heading the first goal from a Taylor corner, he added the other two from Bromley centre's after half-time.

Thus Southampton were sunk without trace, despite playing clever football only to throw away scoring chances. Chivers was a fraction out on three occasions and O'Brien extended Hopkinson more than once.

The Wanderers' midfield resistance was weak and they had Freddie Hill to thank for a top-class performance. New boy Barry Fry, in for the injured Francis Lee, struggled to make an impact on the right. On the other hand Bolton had punch because, Davies apart, they had plenty of threat on the left from Taylor.

Hill brought the house down with a long dribble and running drive at 30 yards which Hollowbread did well to reach and put round the post. Hatton, although loose with some of his clearances, also played with great gusto despite the adroit moves of Terry Paine who was the visitors' main creator.

Davies kept up his run of scoring in every game by finding the net in the 13th minute. His other goals came in the 55th and 78th minutes to complete the first hat-trick by a Wanderer since March 1963.

Bolton Wanderers: Hopkinson; Hartle, Hatton, Rimmer, Edwards, Lennard, Fry, Hill, Davies, Bromley, Taylor.
Southampton: Hollowbread; Williams, Hollywood, Wimshurst, Knapp, Huxford, Paine, O'Brien, Chivers, McGuigan, Sydenham.

Attendance: 10,943
Referee: K.Stokes (Newark)

Giantkillers

22 January 1966
BOLTON WANDERERS 3 WEST BROMWICH ALBION 0

Bolton Wanderers completed their first giantkilling act for 31 years with a well-earned win over First Division West Brom in the third round of the FA Cup.

Francis Lee, scored twice in the Cup victory over First Division West Brom.

It was the fifth Cup meeting with the Midlands side and the first time that Bolton had finished as winners.

Fog creeping in from the surrounding areas at midday became the one threat to the game. The well-sanded ground was hard with moisture seeping up under the influence of the thaw.

Almost from the kick-off Lee was brought down heavily by Fairfax as he tried to take through a pass by Davies. From the free-kick Lee's low shot turned back to Hatton who raced through and, with only Potter to beat, saw his shot rebound off the advancing goalkeeper.

Bolton went ahead in the 27th minute. Fairfax, Albion's left-back, under pressure, made a poor back pass and Bromley fastened on to the ball before Potter could get near it to score.

Just before half-time a corner-kick fell to the Wanderers on the left. When Taylor's cross came over Lee cracked in a hard right-foot shot which was charged down. Regaining possession Lee hit a low left-foot drive which entered the net through a crowd of defenders.

Soon after the interval Hopkinson had to catch a long kick from right-back Cram, one for the few occasions he had to handle the ball.

After 68 minutes a third goal came with a brilliant individual effort by Lee,

who ran on to a pass on the right without being challenged and then cut inside, beating three men, before neatly placing the ball in the net.

It was a great tonic for the crowd but Albion were not taking their impending defeat with very good grace and the referee was not controlling things too well. Crawford went close to getting a consolation goal for Albion near the end, but by then the Wanderers were already worthy winners.

For the second successive season Preston North End were to be the opponents in the fourth round – the Lillywhites winning through after a replay at Deepdale.

Bolton Wanderers: Hopkinson; Hartle, Farrimond, Rimmer, Napier, Hatton, Lee, Bromley, Davies, Hill, Taylor.
West Bromwich Albion: Potter; Cram, Fairfax, Lovett, Jones, Fraser, Brown, Crawford, Kaye, Hope, Clark.

Attendance: 24,425
Referee: J.E.Thacker (Scarborough)

Arsenal brought the big time back to Burnden in February 1967 in the fourth round of the FA Cup. The game ended scoreless but the Gunners won the replay.

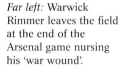

Left: Freddie Hill – hit the net in a memorable League Cup win over Liverpool.

Hill Hijacks Liverpool in League Cup
27 September 1967
BOLTON WANDERERS 3 LIVERPOOL 2

The Wanderers had sprung something of a surprise a fortnight earlier by drawing 1-1 at Anfield in the second round of the League Cup, but the replay at Burnden Park really was a night to remember. The game's fortunes fluctuated tantalisingly with the Wanderers dominating the early stages, losing their grip towards half-time, then regaining command midway through the second half.

Liverpool's downfall began in the 26th minute when Gerry Byrne failed to cut out a Freddie Hill pass and Dave Hatton ran the ball through the penalty area to the by-line. The Wanderers skipper's first shot was beaten out by Tommy Lawrence but Hatton headed the rebound across the face of goal which fell to the eager Gordon Taylor who made no mistake.

Ten minutes from half-time the First Division side got back into it when Tommy Smith converted a penalty awarded after Peter Thompson had been brought down. It was a bad time for Bolton to concede a goal but they withstood tremendous pressure to go in at half-time all square.

Tommy Lawrence repelled a Wanderers revival but he could only parry a powerful shot from Francis Lee in the 70th minute. Hill followed up to plant the ball in the net to put Bolton ahead.

Liverpool hit back and Ian St John was only inches wide with a stinging shot after a shrewd back pass from Tony Hateley. There were 15 minutes remaining when Taylor sprinted inside a defender to latch on to yet another pinpoint pass from Hill. The winger looked up and screwed his shot past a bemused Lawrence.

113

Five minutes later the visitors made it an exciting finale when Ian Callaghan released a 'banana shot' that bent around a wall of astonished Wanderers defenders and curved in the net.

It was an anxious final ten minutes for Bolton but they hung on to register their first giantkilling act in the League Cup competition. In the next round Bolton came up against another First Division side in West Ham, who ran out 4-1 winners at Upton Park.

Bolton Wanderers: Hopkinson; Hatton, Farrimond, Greaves, Hulme, Lennard, Lee, Bromley, Byrom, Hill, Taylor.

Liverpool: Lawrence; Lawler, Byrne, Smith, Yeats, Hughes, Callaghan, Hunt, Hateley, St John, Thompson.

Attendance: 30,669
Referee: J.Finney (Wellington)

High Five
28 October 1967
BOLTON WANDERERS 5 DERBY COUNTY 3

It was a transitional period for the Wanderers who had recently sold Francis Lee to Manchester City and recruited Gareth Williams from Cardiff City. Indeed the visit of Derby for this Second Division game saw Williams playing his third game for the club, a run which had prompted a mini-revival after four straight defeats.

In this eight-goal thriller it was Derby, in their first season under Brian Clough, who went ahead after 12 minutes when Alan Durban found the net at the second attempt after his initial cross-cum-shot had been blocked.

Bolton, stung by the set-back, stormed into action by piling on the pressure and it was Williams who started the move which led to the equaliser after 16 minutes. He combined with Freddie Hill to get in a cross that deflected off a ruck of Derby defenders to John Byrom who brought it under control and steered it into the net.

Four minutes later County 'keeper Reg Matthews failed to collect a left-wing corner and Byrom took advantage to nod the ball home. The Rams struck back after half-time and levelled in the 53rd minute when John O'Hare beat Warwick Rimmer to send a short chip past Hopkinson.

On the hour Gordon Taylor bobbed up on the right to cross for Williams to score his first goal in a Bolton shirt. Six minutes later the Wanderers got a fourth and again credit was largely due to Taylor. He sprinted 25 yards past Peter Daniel to cross the ball hard and low; it fell for Roy Greaves to plant it firmly into goal.

At the other end Durban was just wide with a good effort but Bolton, inspired by success, made it five when Williams cleverly evaded a tackle and crashed the ball home from 30 yards.

Just when it looked as if the Wanderers were coasting Derby sprang back with a super goal. Winger Gordon Hughes worked his way past Farrimond and Hulme before crossing into the penalty area where Kevin Hector was waiting to hit it on the turn past the advancing Hopkinson.

Bolton Wanderers: Hopkinson; Hatton, Farrimond, Williams, Hulme, Rimmer, Bromley, Greaves, Byrom, Hill, Taylor, Sub: Lennard.

Derby County: Matthews; Wright, Daniel, Webster, McFarland, Saxton, Hughes, Durban, O'Hare, Hector, Hinton, Sub: Barker.

Attendance: 12,631
Referee: J.Partridge (Middlesbrough)

Back From the Dead
13 August 1969
BOLTON WANDERERS 6 ROCHDALE 3

In the first round stage of the League Cup for the first time since 1961, the Wanderers produced a magnificent comeback in a game of fluctuating fortunes after Third Division Rochdale gave Bolton more than a fright when they stormed into a 3-1 half-time lead.

Former Wanderer Dennis Butler put them ahead in the 30th minute from a Reg Jenkins pass following a free-kick on the right. Jenkins hit the second with a cannonball free-kick from 30 yards before John Byrom got Bolton off the mark with a goal in the 38th minute.

Rochdale were soon two goals in front again when Eddie Hopkinson misjudged a cross and Butler hammered the ball home. The interval gave the crowd a chance to get their breath back before the goals flowed again.

Three minutes after the restart, Dave Hatton was fouled and Terry Wharton put away the penalty-kick and from this point on, despite a vulnerable defence, Bolton got on top.

Hatton and Greaves set up Byrom's equaliser in the 53rd minute and six minutes later Roy Greaves made it 4-3. Greaves grabbed a fifth for the Wanderers in the 69th minute and with ten minutes left Byrom completed his second hat-trick of the week from a John Ritson cross.

Although that was the end of the scoring it wasn't the end of the excitement. In the 85th minute Rochdale were awarded a penalty for handball by Ritson. Hopkinson, who

Rochdale struck the Wanderers' bar whilst both sides made clearances off their own goal-line.

In the next round the goals dried up as Rotherham United visited Burnden for a scoreless draw. The Yorkshire side finally ended Bolton's interest in the competition in a second replay at Millmoor.

Bolton Wanderers: Hopkinson; Ritson, Hallows, Rimmer, Hurley, Marsh, Wharton, Byrom, Greaves, Hatton, Phillips. Sub: Taylor.

Rochdale: Harker; Smith, Ryder, Melledew, Parry, Ashworth, Whitehead, Rudd, Buck, Jenkins, Butler. Sub: Riley.

Attendance: 10,097

Referee: D.J.Lyden (Birmingham)

Above: John Byrom scored a hat-trick against Rochdale in the League Cup.

Right: Roy Greaves netted twice as the Dale were hit for six.

had not had a happy evening, covered himself with glory when he saved the spot-kick from Jenkins.

As well as the glut of goals, there were plenty of goalmouth incidents,

Goals Galore

29 November 1969
BOLTON WANDERERS 6 QUEEN'S PARK RANGERS 4

One point from the previous five Second Division games and no goals in the last three. That was all the Wanderers had to show as they dropped into one of the relegation spots prior to facing promotion-chasing Queen's Park Rangers at Burnden.

Indeed this was the club's worst-ever Football League position at the time. In contrast, the Londoners had reached the quarter-finals of the Football League Cup, before going out at Manchester City, and had lost once in their previous half-dozen League games.

Rangers arrived to find Burnden frost-bound, making the ball difficult to control and things looked bleak for Bolton when the visitors went ahead after only 45 seconds. Inside-forward Mick Leach headed past Alan Boswell after a pin-point free-kick from Rodney Marsh.

Wanderers' goal famine ended in the 24th minute when Gordon Taylor equalised and, two minutes from the interval, John Byrom grabbed his ninth League goal of the season to put the Trotters in front.

The second half was a real goal feast with end-to-end action to warm up the crowd. John Manning headed Wanderers third goal after 51 minutes but within seconds Barry Bridges kept Rangers in it with their second.

Terry Wharton scored his seventh goal of the season in the 55th minute to restore the Trotters' advantage, only for Rangers full-back, Dave Clement, who was to sign for Bolton almost ten years later, to slam in a Mike Ferguson corner.

Manning headed his second in the 71st minute past a bemused Alan Spratley in the Rangers goal, whilst Byrom made it half a dozen for Bolton with nine minutes remaining and the points were surely safe.

Rangers, however, had the final word when Rodney Marsh clipped one in after 84 minutes to round off the scoring.

This was the Wanderers' highest score since defeating Hull 6-1 at Burnden in August 1967 and the first 6-4 result on the ground since Arsenal had won by that score on Christmas Day 1952.

The victory over Rangers set Bolton off on an undefeated run of six League games without defeat but the Wanderers did have the Indian sign over Rangers that term. The following March, they visited Loftus Road on the back of four straight defeats and were once again staring relegation in the face. This time they registered their best away win of the term – two goals by Roger Hunt and one each from Roy Greaves and John Byrom earning a 4-0 win.

Only one defeat in the final seven games meant Wanderers avoided relegation whilst Rangers missed out in their promotion quest.

Bolton Wanderers: Boswell; Ritson, Hallows, Rimmer, Hurley, Marsh, Wharton, Byrom, Manning, Greaves, Taylor. Sub: Seddon.
Queen's Park Rangers: Spratley; Clement, Harris, Venables, Hunt, Hazell, Ferguson, Leach, Clarke, Marsh, Bridges. Sub: Francis.

Attendance: 7,253
Referee: J.Thacker (Scarborough)

Opposite page, bottom: The Wanderers and Millwall line up to congratulate 'keeper Eddie Hopkinson on his 500th League appearance for Bolton on the opening day of the 1969-70 season.

John Byrom controls the ball on a frosty Burnden pitch during the ten-goal thriller with Queen's Park Rangers.

Roger Hunt came to Burnden from Liverpool in December 1969. Here he runs out with Terry Wharton and John Ritson before a 1-1 draw with Huddersfield the following month.

Kids Kill Blades' Promotion Hopes

16 January 1971
BOLTON WANDERERS 2 SHEFFIELD UNITED 1

After a run of seven League and Cup games without a win and relegation from Division Two staring Bolton in the face, a team with an average age of 20 was fielded against promotion-chasing Sheffield United. Jimmy Meadows had been appointed team manager the day before but the side had been selected by Nat Lofthouse.

There were no less than seven teenagers, Don McAllister and Paul Jones being only 17, the latter making his League debut.

The Burnden Babes fell behind after only 95 seconds. Paul Jones and Bill Dearden chased a long pass deep in the Wanderers' territory. The Sheffield man got his foot to it and John Tudor came

in to hit the ball into an empty net after Alan Boswell had come off his line.

This did not deter the youngsters who hit back with a display of all action football, never letting the visitors settle on the ball. The equaliser came after 19 minutes play. Ian Seddon started it by picking up the ball in midfield and playing it out to Garry Jones on the left. He pushed a pass inside and Seddon, who had made ground to the edge of the United penalty area, shot past Alan Hodgkinson for his first goal of the season.

This was a tremendous boost for the youngsters who began to thrill the crowd but were unlucky to have a goal from Paul Fletcher disallowed.

The second half continued in the same vein, Ron Phillips hitting the post with a left-foot drive from an acute angle. The deciding goal came 11 minutes from time. Paul Jones cleared the ball deep into United territory, Fletcher chased after it and, as Hodgkinson raced from his goal, the young centre-

Bolton reverted to an all-white kit for 1969-70. This lasted for two seasons. This is the squad for 1970-71 that suffered relegation to Division Three. Back row (left to right): W.Rimmer, A.Boswell, J.Ritson, T.Wharton, S.Farrimond. Middle row: J.Manning, J.Byrom, A.Marsh, J.Hulme, P.Fletcher, I.Seddon. Front row: R.Phillips, G.Taylor, R.Greaves, R.Hunt, C.Hurley, G.Williams.

Left: Manager Nat Lofthouse surveys Burnden Park in 1969.

Ian Seddon
levels the
score against
the Blades. It
was Bolton's
last victory in
Division Two
before
relegation.

forward slipped the ball past him from the edge of the area.

As it hit the back of the net Burnden Park erupted. Sadly this was to be the last joyous moment of the 1970-71 season as the final 16 games went by without a win, culminating in relegation to Division Three for the first time in the club's history.

Bolton Wanderers: Boswell; Ritson, McAllister, Waldron, Hulme, Paul Jones, Redfern, Seddon, Fletcher, Garry Jones, Phillips. Sub: Hallows.
Sheffield United: Hodgkinson; Badger, Hemsley, Powell, Colquhoun, Barnwell, Woodward, Tudor, Dearden, Currie, Salmons. Sub: Buckley.

Attendance: 10,146
Referee: P.Baldwin (Middlesbrough)

Oh Garry, Oh Garry Garry Jones…
5 October 1971
BOLTON WANDERERS 3 MANCHESTER CITY 0

Having accounted for First Division Huddersfield Town in the second round of the League Cup at Leeds Road, the Wanderers rose magnificently to the occasion in defeating star-studded Manchester City at Burnden in the third round.

City – League champions, FA Cup winners, League Cup winners and European Cup-winners' Cup winners in recent seasons – fielded three Bolton old boys in their side. Freddie Hill, Wyn Davies and Francis Lee were welcomed by a Burnden crowd of 42,039, the best on the ground whilst the Wanderers were a Third Division club.

The undoubted hero of the game, though, was 20-year-old Garry Jones who notched a hat-trick to become the golden boy of the Wanderers. In defence it was the irrepressible Warwick Rimmer who made sure Francis Lee was kept under wraps. And this after Rimmer almost missed the game, getting caught in traffic he had to run to get to the ground in time for the team-sheet to be handed in.

The Wanderers went ahead after 16 minutes. Alan Waldron floated the ball across from the right and Jones outjumped the City defence to get in a header that was out of Joe Corrigan's reach.

Corrigan made super saves from both John Byrom and John Hulme before Bolton's only moment of defensive uncertainty during the first half. From Mike Summerbee's corner, Charlie Wright missed his punch and Davies lobbed the ball across the face of goal, fortunately Ian Seddon was on hand to head to safety.

City opened the second half brightly but they soon faded away and in the 65th minute the Wanderers went further ahead. Roy Greaves floated the ball forward and Jones raced clear catching the City defence square. Corrigan advanced and although he managed to touch Jones' lob, the ball bounced over the line.

Eleven minutes from time the tie was put beyond any doubt. Waldron was brought down by Willie Donachie inside the penalty area and Jones stepped up to send Corrigan the wrong way with his kick.

So Jones became the hat-trick hero but on this evening every Bolton player was a hero. In the next round the Wanderers drew another successful Cup side in Chelsea at Stamford

Bridge. A 1-1 draw meant another Cup night at Burnden but unfortunately on this occasion the Wanderers went down 6-0 – their heaviest home defeat in the competition.

Bolton Wanderers: Wright; Ritson, Mowbray, Waldron, Hulme, Rimmer, Nicholson, Seddon, Garry Jones, Greaves, Byrom. Sub: Hunt.
Manchester City: Corrigan; Book, Donachie, Doyle, Booth, Towers, Summerbee, Jeffries, Davies, Lee, Hill. Sub: Mellor.

Attendance: 42,039
Referee: K.Styles (Barnsley)

Wanderers on the eve of the 1971-72 season. Back row (left to right): J.Ritson, P.Jones, G.Rowe, A.Marsh, H.Mowbray, P.Hallows. Middle row: P.Nicholson, D.McAllister, C.Wright, R.Greaves, A.Boswell, J.Byrom, G.Williams, W.Rimmer. Front row: A.Waldron, J.Redfern, I.Seddon, J.Armfield (manager), J.Hulme, G.Jones, R.Phillips.

They All Count!
25 November 1972
BOLTON WANDERERS 2 ROTHERHAM UNITED 1

An unforgettable promotion-winning season saw the Wanderers lift the Third Division championship after only two terms under Jimmy Armfield. Bolton's home form throughout the season was superb, only one League defeat, by 1-0 at the hands of fellow promotion chasers Blackburn, which attracted a crowd of 33,010.

The visit of Rotherham United, however, not only almost put the home record under pressure, but one of the most bizarre goals ever scored on the ground proved to be the winner.

Players struggled to keep their feet in the treacherous conditions, table-topping Bolton not getting any fluency into their game in the early stages, although a John

Byrom pile driver was blocked after he had dribbled past a couple of defenders to get into a shooting position.

Then United 'keeper Jim McDonagh, later to ply his trade regularly at Burnden, failed to hold a Byrom shot and a tremendous scramble developed. Both Stuart Lee and Garry Jones were pushed over but the referee waved play on despite of loud appeals for a penalty.

Rotherham then took the lead in the 38th minute with their first real shot at goal. The ball came in from the left and the unmarked Trevor Womble had time to pull the ball down and crack a left-foot shot into the net. Just before the interval McDonagh failed to hold a Ronnie Phillips inswinging corner and Byrom forced it into the net. The joy was short-lived as a linesman's flag was raised and the referee awarded a free-kick to the visitors.

Rain continued to pour down during the second half as Bolton began to have a desperate look about them. Ian Seddon came on for the injured Don McAllister and with his first touch he started the move that brought about the 68th minute equaliser. Seddon won the ball midway inside the Rotherham half and passed it forward to Lee. He hit a left-foot shot across goal for Byrom to side foot into the net from point-blank range.

Then, as the game seemed to be heading for a draw, with only four minutes left, came an incredible goal that earned Bolton the points. Rotherham's 'keeper, McDonagh, seemed to have assumed the ball had crossed the goal-line for a goal-kick. He placed the ball and turned to make his run up. As he did so Garry Jones ran up to slot it into the empty net with the referee waving play on. Although Rotherham protested to both the referee and the linesman, the goal stood to keep Bolton on top of the Third Division.

Bolton Wanderers: Wright; Ritson, McAllister, Rimmer, P.Jones, Nicholson, Byrom, G.Jones, Greaves, Lee, Phillips. Sub: Seddon for McAllister.
Rotherham United: McDonagh; Houghton, Breckin, Wilkinson, Mielczarek, Swift, Bentley, Ham, Womble, Stowell, Muller. Sub: Gilbert for Ham.

Attendance: 7,980
Referee: T.H.C.Reynolds (Swansea)

The Bluebirds' Late, Late Cup Reprieve
3 February 1973
BOLTON WANDERERS 2 CARDIFF CITY 2

Referee Ted Wallace was at the middle of a Cup storm at this exciting FA Cup fourth-round tie that ended in dramatic fashion with an equalising goal from Cardiff in the sixth minute of injury time of a game that lasted 97 minutes. After 88 minutes he ordered off Wanderers' veteran skipper Warwick Rimmer along with Cardiff's Welsh international Gil Reece for nothing more than exuberance. And, after appearing to give a penalty to the Welshmen, consulted his linesman and gave Bolton a free-kick.

Third Division Wanderers, having conceded only five goals at home all season, looked well on the road to victory in the 40th minute. A disastrous mistake by Cardiff right-back Phil Dwyer left Garry Jones with the formality of nodding the ball into an empty net. Although midfield man Billy Kellock caused problems for Bolton. Cardiff's Irish 'keeper Bill Irwin made a string of fine saves, including one out of this world effort from a savage John Ritson drive.

Second Division Cardiff looked as though they were on their way out, but in the 80th minute, a John Vincent free-kick bobbed about in the Bolton goalmouth before being half-cleared to Kellock, who lashed a low drive that gave 'keeper Charlie Wright no chance.

Six minutes later a blistering 25-yard effort from Ritson put the Wanderers

Wanderers before the start of the 1972-73 season. At the end of it they were Third Division champions: Back row (left to right): A.Waldron, A.Parkinson, J.Redfern, P.Olinyk, C.Duffey, J.Ritson, P.Hallows. Middle row: P.Nicholson, P.Jones, C.Wright, S.Allardyce, B.Siddall, R.Wright, G.Jones. Front row: D.McAllister, S.Lee, R.Greaves, H.Mowbray, W.Rimmer, J.Byrom, I.Seddon, R.Phillips.

Right: Ticket from the Cardiff game.

2-1 ahead and it looked all over. Unfortunately, Bolton lost a certain fifth-round place because they lacked the composure needed to slow down those closing minutes.

The dismissals came after a great save by Wright that ended with him stunned in the back of his own net whilst play continued. Finally a 96th minute deflection off Don McAllister gave Leighton Phillips Cardiff's

second equaliser with Wright helpless from his 20-yard effort.

The replay at Ninian Park also ended all-square but the Wanderers finally reached the fifth round, for the first time since 1965, with a 1-0 second replay win at The Hawthorns. A crowd of 39,556 were at Burnden for the next tie against Second Division Luton Town. Unfortunately they ended the Cup dream with a 1-0 win but a more important prize was secured at the end of the season – the Third Division championship.

Bolton Wanderers: Wright; Ritson, McAllister, Rimmer, P.Jones, Waldron, Byrom, G.Jones, Greaves, Lee, R.Phillips.
Cardiff City: Irwin; Dwyer, Bell, L.Phillips, Murray, Powell, Reece, McCulloch, Kellock, Vincent, Rees.
Attendance: 24,729
Referee: E.Wallace (Crewe)

BOLTON WANDERERS FOOTBALL & ATHLETIC CO. LTD.
BURNDEN PARK

F.A. CUP — 4th ROUND

BOLTON v. CARDIFF CITY
SATURDAY, FEBRUARY 3rd, 1973.
KICK-OFF 3-00 p.m.

Centre Stand 65p
Block B   Row R   Seat 133

Will All Ticket Holders please note the Plan on other side of ticket and go through the appropriate turnstile

This ticket is issued on the understanding that the holder occupies the seat 30 minutes before time of kick-off.

In the event of postponement this ticket will be valid for the re-arranged date. NO MONEY REFUNDED.

This Portion to be Retained

Byrom is the Sunday Saviour
6 January 1974
BOLTON WANDERERS 3 STOKE CITY 2

Quick thinking Bolton Wanderers made football history by arranging the first major professional match on a Sunday. Within a few hours of hearing unofficially about the FA's decision to allow Sunday play in the third round of the FA Cup, Bolton had switched their game against Stoke. Whilst other clubs wrestled with the variety of problems involved, pacesetters Bolton had consulted Stoke, who immediately agreed to the switch.

They then sought legal advice on the Sunday Observance Act and began to explore the most convenient way of admitting fans to Burnden Park whilst at the same time complying with the law.

Sunday soccer, with all its attendant vices and virtues, kicked-off to a disappointing shower of rain but this failed to dampen the fire of those who would have the Sabbath kept holy with placards proclaiming 'Death is sure' and 'Christ is the Answer'.

Fans cheerfully paid 40p or 60p for team-sheets that gained them admission – no one was allowed to buy a ticket – but the Lord's Day Observance Society claimed that the game constituted a disregard of the law of God and the law of the land. Wanderers officials, however, claimed that because of the law of the land at the time – namely a three-day week – many regular supporters would have been unable to watch a Saturday game.

Whatever the arguments, Soccer on a Sunday was voted an overwhelming success by the 39,138 crowd – twice as big as Burnden's best in that season to date – over three times better than the average attendance and the best single gate of the entire third round.

The game belonged to John Byrom and his hat-trick knocked out First

Wanderers before the start of the 1973-74 season. Back row (left to right): I.Seddon, J.Ritson, R.Greaves, P.Jones, B.Siddall, C.Wright, P.Nicholson, D.McAllister, G.Jones, M.McBurney. Front row: P.Hallows, N.Whatmore, A.Dunne, W.Rimmer, J.Armfield (manager), S.Lee, R.Phillips, A.Waldron, J.Byrom.

It's the John Byrom show. He celebrates his first, knocks home the second and volley's the third as Stoke are beaten on a Sunday.

Division Stoke, in a Sunday spectacular. His first goal arrived in the 25th minute when Garry Jones put over a cross that eluded Paul Jones and bounced for Byrom to stoop to head home.

The second came just after the interval when he sent a blistering shot under Stoke goalkeeper John Farmer after he had run their defence ragged. In the 62nd minute his third perhaps summed up Byrom. He received a pass from Peter Thompson before casually flicking the ball up to fire home a left-foot half volley.

From then on Stoke turned the tables to hit back with two goals. In the 64th minute John Ritchie hit home a shot from the edge of the area and then, in the 85th minute, John Ritson brought down Ritchie in the area. Substitute Sean Haslegrave converted the kick to make it 3-2 to the Wanderers, who had Byrom to thank for clearing off his own goal-line to deny Stoke a replay.

An evangelist claimed it was 'a Godless day' and quoted the second book of *Samuel*, Chapter 19, Verse 2: 'And the victory that day turned into mourning'. His sentiments were probably echoed by the Stoke fans on their way back to the Potteries of course, Wanderers supporters going home for a late Sunday lunch would not believe it.

Bolton Wanderers: Siddall; Ritson, Nicholson, Rimmer, P.Jones, Waldron, Byrom, G.Jones, Greaves, Whatmore, Thompson. Sub: Lee for Rimmer.
Stoke City: Farmer; Dodd, Pejic, Skeels, Smith, Bloor, Robertson, Greenhoff, Ritchie, Hurst, Mahoney. Sub: Haslegrave for Hurst.

Attendance: 39,138
Referee: H.Hackney (Barnsley)

Champions Have no Answer to Burnden Strikeforce

15 April 1974
BOLTON WANDERERS 2 MIDDLESBROUGH 1

A fantasy goal from John Byrom kept alive the Wanderers' faint chances of joining Middlesbrough in the First Division the following term. Byrom, back after a three-match injury lay-off, bounced back into the Burnden limelight to put the Wanderers on their way to a 2-1 victory over the Second Division champions. He picked the ball up on the edge of the 'Boro area in the 18th minute, dribbled past three defenders when it seemed impossible to find a way through. Even to fail then would have been an achievement but

Byrom raced on to crack the ball home before raising an arm to salute in typical 'J.B.' fashion.

And so, in fairy-tale style, Byrom's 24th goal of the season crowned his return to a side which had scored only once in the previous three games without him. It also put Bolton on course to being the first team to take four points from Middlesbrough.

Jack Charlton's side, top of the League since the previous September, could be forgiven a lacklustre approach but this was not the case. Indeed, but for an

Wanderers in August 1974: Back row (left to right): A.Waldron, N.Whatmore, B.Siddall, G.Jones, R.Greaves. Middle row: M.Walsh, P.Jones, J.Byrom, S.Allardyce, P.Nicholson, H.Curran. Front row: S.Lee, P.Thompson, J.Ritson, P.Reid, A.Dunne.

autumn slump, the Wanderers themselves would have been hot on the heels of 'Boro's runaway success.

Bolton's second goal in the 51st minute had quality too. Winger Peter Thompson, whose arrival sparked the season into life, sent over a perfect cross and Garry Jones did it justice by timing his leap to perfection to give 'keeper Pat Cuff no chance.

The Wanderers had a good chance to go further ahead when Sam Allardyce received an Alan Waldron free-kick only to head over from a good position. Middlesbrough had a lot of possession late in the game without being able to prise open the Bolton defence until four minutes from time.

Then, Stuart Boam scrambled home,

but it was too late for the visitors to stave off their fourth League defeat of the season. For Burnden's second highest League attendance of the term this proved to be the peak as the final two games ended in defeat without a goal being scored.

Bolton Wanderers: Siddall; Ritson, Nicholson, McAllister, Allardyce, Waldron, Olinyk, G.Jones, Byrom, Whatmore, Thompson.
Middlesbrough: Cuff; Craggs, Creamer, Souness, Boam, Madden, Murdoch, Mills, Hickton, Foggon, Armstrong. Sub: Brine for Foggon.

Attendance: 22,246
Referee: H.G.New (Bristol)

Super Sam ...Bionic Man
27 December 1975
BOLTON WANDERERS 2 SUNDERLAND 1

The crowd of 42,680 for Wanderers' Division Two clash with Sunderland

was the biggest for a League game at Burnden since September 1962 when

Manchester United visited. Indeed, the crowd was topped on the day only by those at Manchester United, Leeds and Liverpool.

At kick-off time many were still outside the ground as the game that saw no holds barred, no prisoners taken and football of the highest quality, began. The opening half belonged to League leaders Sunderland. The Roker side, full of skill and character, could have had at least three goals to add to the messy affair that put them ahead on the stroke of half-time.

The boost they had been chasing came when Wanderers' full-back Tony Dunne was barged into a Tony Towers free-kick to send the ball past Barry Siddall.

Sunderland's good fortune turned after the interval when the Wanderers began to take command with the visitors keen to sit on their slender lead. The game was played at a fast pace and this all-out work rate was reinforced by some ferocious tackling.

Yet no amount of defensive legislation in the world could have counteracted Sam Allardyce's brilliantly headed equaliser when he rose between Joe Bolton and Jack Ashurst. The ball flew past Jim Montgomery and Burnden erupted to celebrate a classic goal.

The Wanderers then stepped up the pressure and got the winner to end the contest and go joint leaders with the Roker side. John Byrom, who was playing his first full game after injury, was the hero with his fifth goal of the season. He darted forward to head home a Peter Thompson cross, the winger also returning to the side after injury.

Sunderland had lacked the killer instinct during their best spell whilst Bolton took full advantage of opportunities that fell their way.

Bolton Wanderers: Siddall; Ritson, Dunne, Greaves, P.Jones, Allardyce, Byrom, Whatmore, G.Jones, Reid, Thompson.
Sunderland: Montgomery; Malone, Bolton, Towers, Clarke, Ashurst, Kerr, Finney, Holden, Robson, Henderson.
Attendance: 42,680
Referee: K.W.Ridden (Shrewsbury)

FA Cup Extravaganza
14 February 1976
BOLTON WANDERERS 3 NEWCASTLE UNITED 3

The Wanderers prepared for this FA Cup fifth-round tie with a mid-season break to Torremolinos, while Newcastle United's manager Gordon Lee put the

Garry Jones makes it 2-2 in an epic FA Cup-tie with Newcastle United.

confrontation into prospective by claiming that his side were not just taking on a team but the whole town.

Newcastle were unbeaten in Cup football that term having already reached the League Cup Final, whilst the Wanderers were heading the Second Division. Twice Bolton came back from 'the dead' to force a replay after one of the most exciting, energy-sapping, lung-bursting Cup-ties that the club had ever been involved in.

It all looked so rosy for the Wanderers in the early stages, going ahead after five minutes when Sam Allardyce headed home Peter Thompson's cross. Newcastle's midfield inspiration Tommy Cassidy sent Malcolm Macdonald away and he outpaced the Bolton defence before rounding Barry Siddall for the equaliser.

A minute before half-time, United went ahead with a goal from Macdonald that had Burnden Park buzzing with excitement. The striker had his back to the Bolton goal when he collected a throw-in from Tommy Craig. He dummied Paul Jones, swivelled and hammered a fantastic bending shot with his right foot high into the top corner of the net from 25 yards. Wanderers manager Ian Greaves later came out with his memorable quote "I can only blame the tea lady for that goal. You certainly couldn't blame any of our players." Bolton took the fight to Newcastle and made it 2-2 in the 51st minute. Roy Greaves stabbed the ball into the danger area and it was deflected to Garry Jones to score from close range. There were eight minutes left on the clock when Newcastle looked to have sewn it up with a third goal. Cassidy sent Gowling through the middle and the striker, who used to play for Ian Greaves at Huddersfield and was later to come to Burnden, made no mistake.

The drama was still to come, however. Within three minutes Paul Jones galloped up to meet a Greaves corner and powered in a header which went through Macdonald's legs and over the line for a spectacular ending to a memorable game.

There were to be two more Cup classics with Newcastle, a scoreless draw at St James' Park before the First Division side ran out 2-1 winners in a second replay at Elland Road.

Bolton Wanderers: Siddall; Ritson, Dunne, Greaves, P.Jones, Allardyce, Byrom, Whatmore, G.Jones, Reid, Thompson.
Newcastle United: Mahoney, Nattrass, Kennedy, Nulty, Keeley, Howard, Burns, Cassidy, Macdonald, Gowling, Craig. Sub: Barrowclough for Nulty.

Attendance: 46,584
Referee: J.Homewood (Sunbury on Thames)

Watched by Peter Reid, Steve Taylor nets the first equaliser in the controversial League Cup-tie against Fulham.

Walsh Earns League Cup Replay
5 October 1976
BOLTON WANDERERS 2 FULHAM 2 (AFTER EXTRA-TIME)

This was 'the evening that time stood still at Burnden', enabling the Wanderers to hit a 96th-minute equaliser that was to keep them in the League Cup amid incredible scenes in this third-round replay. Bobby Moore was sent off and then the entire Fulham team walked off at the end of normal time. To get the game restarted, referee Kevin McNally, a linesman and two policemen had to make an impassioned appeal at the dressing-room door.

A minute later Fulham made their reappearance led by coach Bobby Campbell, furious because they felt that Bolton's second goal had been scored long after the match should have ended. There were practically no stoppages and Moore felt he had a point to make to the referee and was dismissed for doing so – and as he disappeared down the tunnel his colleagues began to follow him.

The equaliser that started the fury came from Mike Walsh. He lobbed the ball over the head of 'keeper Peter Mellor after Fulham had withstood tremendous pressure in the second half.

The Londoners had taken a 32nd minute lead when John Mitchell collected a cross from Ernie Howe. Wanderers 'keeper Jim McDonagh came hurtling out as Mitchell shot low into the bottom corner.

Bolton equalised three minutes before the interval. Peter Nicholson's blasted free-kick from the edge of the penalty area was only half blocked by Mellor and Steve Taylor followed up to hit the net from two yards out.

The joy was short-lived as within a minute Fulham regained their lead. Howe became the hero as he headed home after a cross from Moore had been flicked on by John Dowie. Fulham staged a tremendous rearguard action during the second half and looked to be on their way to a fourth-round tie at Swansea until Walsh's late effort.

Extra-time couldn't separate the sides and so a second replay took place at St Andrew's. In an ill-tempered affair, the Wanderers ran out 2-1 winners to continue their best-ever run in the competition until 1994-95.

Bolton Wanderers: McDonagh, Nicholson, Walsh, Greaves, P.Jones, Allardyce, Morgan, Whatmore, Taylor, Reid, Smith. Sub: Waldron.
Fulham: Mellor; Bullivant, Strong, Slough, Howe, Moore, Dowie, Evanson, Mitchell, Lacy, Barrett. Sub: Lloyd for Slough.
Attendance: 15,010
Referee: K.McNally (Hooton)

Wembley Dreams Shattered
15 February 1977
BOLTON WANDERERS 0 EVERTON 1

The Wanderers were on their way to Wembley – or so all their supporters thought after a 1-1 draw in the first leg of the League Cup semi-final at Goodison Park. Unfortunately stage fright caught up with Bolton in the second leg before what was Burnden Park's last attendance of over 50,000.

Everton's first win since Gordon Lee took control was enough to take him to a League Cup Final for the second year in succession. The visitors never looked completely happy – yet they always looked slightly better than the Wanderers who couldn't get their game together for what was probably the worst collective performance of the season.

The only goal came in the 23rd minute. Ronnie Goodlass collected a throw-in and got to the by-line to deliver the perfect cross. The country's most expensive striker, Bob Latchford, climbed to head past Jim McDonagh from five yards.

Everton had the opportunity to make the victory more convincing when they were awarded a 65th-minute penalty after Sam Allardyce had brought down Duncan McKenzie. McKenzie himself got up to take the kick and promptly shot yards wide of McDonagh's right-hand post.

The nervousness of the occasion became contagious as both sides then struggled to find any influence. Bolton couldn't find any rhythm but they did have one magnificent chance to equalise when, just before half-time a clearance by Ken McNaught hit Peter Reid, the ball fell to Neil Whatmore who lobbed over the bar.

Two minutes from time Willie Morgan forced the ball home off David Jones – only to be given offside, and with that went Bolton's Wembley dreams.

The Wanderers were left with some consolation with the news that Second Division leaders Chelsea had lost on the same evening thus increasing promotion hopes. Unfortunately the blow of losing a Cup semi-final proved to be significant in the build up to missing out on promotion by the narrowest of margins for a second successive season.

Bolton Wanderers: McDonagh; Nicholson, Dunne, Greaves, P.Jones, Allardyce, Morgan, Whatmore, G.Jones, Reid, Waldron. Sub: Thompson.
Everton: Lawson, Bernard, D.Jones, Lyons, McNaught, Hamilton, King, Dobson, Latchford, McKenzie, Goodlass.

Attendance: 50,413
Referee: J.K.Taylor (Wolverhampton)

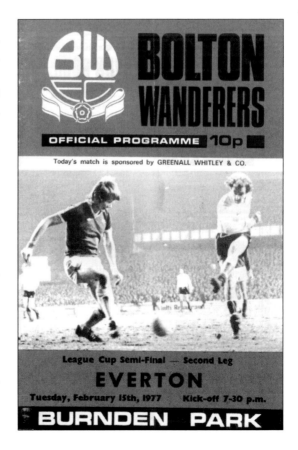

Programme from the game which saw Bolton's Wembley dreams dashed.

Roy Greaves (right) slots home Wanderers' late, late winner against Tottenham.

Roy's Yer Man

26 November 1977

BOLTON WANDERERS 1 TOTTENHAM HOTSPUR 0

A matter of who was the best side in Division Two was partly settled in this tense encounter. The Wanderers took a four-point lead at the top of the table over Spurs in this private battle between the sides with more class than anyone in the Second Division.

The clash was not a classic, too much nervous tension both on and off the field saw to that, but it was still 'edge of the seat' stuff to see two great sides locked in football combat.

Tottenham claimed they were unlucky when, what appeared to be a perfectly good goal by Neil McNab, was disallowed in the 47th minute. The Scot's 25-yard header flew into the net off a post and he went off to celebrate with his teammates not noticing a linesman's flag for offside against John Duncan.

But had Bolton not suffered their share of bad luck during the previous two seasons? Manager Ian Greaves claimed, "This is the new spirit of Bolton. Don't talk to me about Spurs and their good football and their hard luck because we have had all that."

The Wanderers created chances a plenty during the first half but the pendulum appeared to swing the Londoners way just before the interval.

Goalkeeper Jim McDonagh had to turn a header from Duncan on to the crossbar and Spurs continued to cause problems during the second half.

As time wore on the game seemed to be heading for a draw but, in the 89th minute, Roy Greaves popped up 12 yards from goal to shoot past Barry Daines to set Burnden alight. TV's *Match of the Day* viewers were treated to the spectacle later in the evening.

The game certainly took something out of Bolton and they went on to lose three of their next four matches including a League Cup defeat at the hand of Leeds United. This after only one defeat in the opening 19 games. By the New Year the Wanderers were back on track – the turning point being a 2-2 FA Cup third-round draw at Tottenham.

Bolton Wanderers: McDonagh, Nicholson, Dunne, Greaves, P.Jones, Allardyce, Morgan, Whatmore, Walsh, Waldron, Worthington. Sub. Train.
Tottenham Hotspur: Daines; Naylor, Holmes, Hoddle, Osgood, Perryman, Pratt, McNab, Moores, Duncan, Taylor. Sub: Armstrong.

Attendance: 32,266
Referee: A.Chalinor (Maltby)

Walking Wounded Back to Win Cup-tie

10 January 1978
BOLTON WANDERERS 2 TOTTENHAM HOTSPUR 1 (AFTER EXTRA-TIME)

Only seven weeks after a tense League encounter the top two Second Division sides met in the third round of the FA Cup. A crowd of almost 44,000 had witnessed a thriller at White Hart Lane the previous Saturday, Neil Whatmore getting an 86th-minute equaliser to force a 2-2 draw.

The replay at Burnden curiously, began quietly with neither side prepared to commit themselves fully until Bolton began to grind forward with familiar aggression. Fear that the FA Cup may be an intrusion into promotion ambitions did not show as Spurs absorbed the Wanderers' pressure and then broke away to hit the post with an effort from Peter Taylor.

Peter Reid had the ball in the net for Bolton but his effort was ruled out for offside. The deadlock was broken six minutes into the second half with a spectacular goal from full-back John Ritson. Willie Morgan rolled a free-kick square to him and he let fly with such power from 20 yards that 'keeper Barry Daines was left helpless. It was a super sight for Ritson who had only just returned to action after a cartilage operation.

Neil Whatmore's goal-bound header was blocked by Jim Holmes and Daines saved acrobatically from Ray Train, but disaster struck for the Wanderers four minutes from time when Steve Perryman was brought down and Peter Taylor equalised from the penalty spot.

There was no let up in the action during extra-time. The match was to be remembered as Ritson's night when he created the Wanderers' winner seconds before half-time of extra-time. He quickly controlled a pass from Reid out on the right wing, got around Holmes as if he was a natural winger and put over a perfect centre for substitute Garry Jones to hurtle in to head a magnificent goal.

It was also a personal success for Jones who had also recovered from a cartilage operation. The reward for Bolton was a fourth-round home tie against Mansfield Town.

Bolton Wanderers: McDonagh, Ritson, Nicholson, Greaves, Walsh, Allardyce, Morgan, Whatmore, Train, Reid, Worthington. Sub: G.Jones for Greaves.

Tottenham Hotspur: Daines; Naylor, Holmes, Hoddle, McAllister, Perryman, Pratt, McNab, Duncan, Lee, Taylor. Sub: Armstrong for McNab.

Attendance: 31,314

Referee: D.A.G.Nippard (Christchurch)

The headlines after Wanderers' Cup win over Tottenham.

BOLTON'S BIONIC HEROES!

By Bill Elliott

BOLTON'S almost forgotten stars, John Ritson and Garry Jones, last night engineered a memorable F.A. Cup triumph.

In an extra-time thriller at Burnden Park, it was their goals which gave Bolton a 2—1 replay win over Spurs.

Between them, Ritson and Jones have had four cartilage operations in the last 12 months, and the message from both after the game was that they are now ready to add genuine impetus to Bolton's major target—promotion to the First Division.

Said Ritson: "I hope I proved something tonight. I certainly proved something to myself by scoring that goal with the leg that has lost both cartilages. It's been a terrible 12 months, recovering from one operation and then having another one.

"... I knew it was up to ... ... ected at times ... ... the dumps."

COMEBACK STARS ... Bolton goal aces Garry Jones and John Ritson lead the celebrations

Picture: JOHN DAWES

133

The Wanderers celebrate on the steps of Bolton Town Hall after winning the Second Division title.

135

There's Only One Franky Worthy

22 December 1978

BOLTON WANDERERS 3 MANCHESTER UNITED 0

The Wanderers' First Division leading scorer Frank Worthington – his red bandanna more conspicuous than the combined presence of Dave Sexton's 11 Red Devils – set his side on the way to a prestigious victory.

Burnden Park was only passed fit three hours before the kick-off of this First Division match and, whilst others slipped and moved uncertainly, nimble-footed Worthington tore United's defence to shreds. To add to the visitors' shattered title hopes, Bolton's victory was gained with three former Old Trafford heroes.

The old brigade of left-back Tony Dunne and right winger Willie Morgan helped create the breakthrough for Worthington before Alan Gowling, the third member of the ex-United set, hit Bolton's third.

On the skid pan pitch, there seemed to be little danger when Dunne floated a cross into the penalty area. United's centre-half Gordon McQueen was static as Worthington calmly allowed the ball to drop on to his toe to steer the ball past a helpless Gary Bailey.

That breakthrough came after 12 minutes and it wasn't long before Worthington struck again with his 16th goal of the season from a tantalising cross by Morgan. Brian Greenhoff, under pressure from Peter Reid, appeared to handle and, although the referee didn't respond, Worthington picked his spot to leave Bailey bewildered.

United were exposed repeatedly by the Worthington-Gowling spearhead and although they regrouped at half-time it took only five minutes of the second half for Bolton to make it 3-0. It was Worthington who set it up with a quick throw-in to Gowling who chested the ball past two defenders before hitting the net.

In the final minutes Worthington was denied a hat-trick when Martin Buchan cleared off the line, but by then the Wanderers were already celebrating an early Christmas.

The flamboyant striker left Burnden clutching the ball and manager Ian Greaves proclaiming, "Frank was like a cheeky lad playing in a park, everything he tried came off – flicks, backheels – the lot."

In a game that was being choked by faceless regimentation, Worthington had re-emerged to become the most exciting forward in the country. For United, it was the start of four consecutive League defeats and the end of championship aspirations.

Bolton Wanderers: McDonagh, Nicholson, Dunne, Greaves, P.Jones, Walsh, Morgan, Reid, Gowling, Worthington, McNab. Sub: Whatmore.

Manchester United: Bailey, B.Greenhoff, Connell, McIlroy, McQueen, Buchan, Coppell, J.Greenhoff, Ritchie, Macari, Thomas. Sub: Nicholl for J.Greenhoff.

Attendance: 32,390
Referee: P.Partridge (Durham)

Frank Worthington who tore the United defence to shreds.

Opposite page, top: We've done it! Roy Greaves, John Ritson, Tony Dunne, Mike Walsh and Paul Jones accept the crowd's cheers after securing the Second Division championship by drawing 0-0 with Fulham in April 1978.

Opposite page, bottom: Bolton parade the championship trophy before Peter Thompson's testimonial game in May 1978.

The Great Escape

4 May 1982

BOLTON WANDERERS 3 DERBY COUNTY 2

Bolton had one foot in the Third Division after losing 7-1 to FA Cup Finalists Queens Park Rangers at Loftus Road the previous Saturday. Derby came to Burnden three days later in relegation trouble themselves. The Wanderers knew they had to win and then defeat Sheffield Wednesday at Burnden in the last game of the season to stand any chance of staying in the Second Division.

The way Bolton took the points against Derby meant that the débâcle at Loftus Road was soon forgotten as a dramatic last-kick winner from Chris Thompson opened up the escape route amid scenes of excitement and jubilation.

It was just reward for a courageous second-half performance which showed both strength and determination, for Wanderers twice came from behind to clinch a hat-trick of wins over Derby County during 1981-82.

Amazingly, Thompson's winner almost proved the one that got away. The game was deep in injury time and the seconds were ticking away when his first shot hit the legs of the Rams 'keeper Yakka Banovic. When Peter Reid's follow up hit the post, all seemed lost until Thompson popped up to calmly side foot the ball home from a difficult angle.

There wasn't even time to restart the game and Wanderers, who had seen their survival hopes fading with every passing minute, breathed again.

Thompson's soaring header in the 24th minute came after Brian Attley had put Derby ahead. Wanderers' defence was again caught out when

Charlie George was allowed to run free and round Jim McDonagh to finish in easy fashion.

The finale was set up when Tony Henry smashed home his 12th goal of the season in the 57th minute from a free-kick.

It was no evening for the faint-hearted, but having overcome this obstacle, they signed off the season in style by defeating Sheffield Wednesday 3-1 the following Saturday. Even then safety wasn't assured until Cardiff finally ran out of games and fell into Division Three.

Bolton Wanderers: McDonagh; Whitworth, Brennan, Henry, Jones, Doyle, Chandler, Hoggan, Gowling, Reid, Thompson. Sub: Foster.

Derby County: Banovic; Barton, Buckley, Skivington, Sheridan, McAlle, Powell, Attley, George, Swindlehurst, Emson. Sub: Wilson for Barton.

Attendance: 5,226
Referee: G.P.Owen (Anglesey)

Caldwell's Capers Equal Record
10 September 1983
BOLTON WANDERERS 8 WALSALL 1

Tony Caldwell scored a club record of five goals in a Football League game during the 8-1 hammering of Walsall. Here they are.

Tony Caldwell, Bolton's part-time footballer and an electrician by trade, lit up Burnden Park with a personal feast of goalscoring in this Division Three match.

Caldwell, signed at the start of the club's first season in the Third Division for ten years, from Northern Premier League Horwich RMI for £2,000, smacked in five goals. This equalled a club record for a first-class match set by Jim Cassidy in a 13-0 FA Cup victory over Sheffield United at Pikes Lane in 1890.

Caldwell grabbed a hat-trick in 27 minutes of first-half fury, added two more after half-time and could easily have had a couple more.

The Salford-born player began the blitz in the 18th minute when he hammered home a chance from five yards out set up by Warren Joyce. Four minutes later Caldwell beat the entire Walsall defence to an extra-long clearance from 'keeper Simon Farnworth and volleyed in past the stranded Ron Green.

Within seconds the Wanderers were three up. A Caldwell drive was blocked by Green and Ray Deakin darted in to guide the ball into the unguarded net.

A minute from half-time a Jeff Chandler free-kick flicked on by Simon Rudge, found Caldwell at the far post to complete his hat-trick.

Bolton came out for the second half looking for more goals and in the 59th minute a Neil Redfearn shot was only parried by Green into the path of Caldwell who made no mistake.

Twenty minutes later Steve Thompson's corner found Gerry McElhinney at the far post. His header was met nonchalantly by Caldwell to register his fifth.

A 25-yard drive by Rudge took the Wanderers' tally to seven and in the 87th minute centre-half Peter Valentine got his first goal for the club. It was a case of saving the best until last, his thundering left-foot volley would have undoubtedly taken pride of place but for Caldwell's exploits.

In the dying seconds Ally Brown tapped home a consolation for Walsall, but it was enough to deny Bolton the opportunity of equalling their best League victory – the 8-0 success over Barnsley in October 1934. Walsall player-boss Alan Buckley whisked his players off right after the match but must have felt like leaving them to it and catching the first bus home when he took himself off after 62 minutes.

Bolton Wanderers: Farnworth; Borrows, Deakin, Joyce, McElhinney, Valentine, Thompson, Chandler, Rudge, Caldwell, Redfearn. Sub: Foster.
Walsall: Green; Gates, Mower, Shakespeare, Sinnott, Hart, Buckley, Brown, Summerfield, Preece, Brazier. Sub: Jones for Buckley.

Attendance: 4,375
Referee: G.Tyson (Sunderland)

Off the Bottom with Seven Goals

22 September 1984

BOLTON WANDERERS 7 PLYMOUTH ARGYLE 2

Bolton strikers, Tony Caldwell and Jeff Chandler, produced the perfect response after being dropped by manager John McGovern for a mid-

Bolton Wanderers at the start of the 1984-85 season. Back row (left to right): P.Valentine, J.Phillips, M.Came, G.McElhinney, N.Berry, P.Booth, G.Oghani. Middle row: W.Joyce (coach), B.Borrows, S.Thompson, A.Caldwell, S.Farnworth, J.Platt, R.Deakin, P.Lodge, W.Joyce, P.Nightingale (physiotherapist). Front row: W.Foster, C.Wright (first-team coach), J.Chandler, S.Rudge, S.Saunders, J.McGovern (player-manager), G.Bell.

George Oghani slips Bolton's third goal under Plymouth goalkeeper Crudgington.

week defeat at Swansea City. As Wanderers went on a goal romp against bemused Plymouth in this Third Division match, Caldwell cracked in a superb hat-trick and Chandler added two more for Bolton's first home goals of the season.

Within four days of crashing to the bottom of the League, Wanderers hoisted themselves six places with this first victory of the season that inflicted Plymouth's heaviest defeat for 12 years.

The first goal went in from the boot of Warren Joyce after eight minutes as goalkeeper Geoff Crudgington ended up looking as though he was trying to do the hokey-cokey to a low shot that it seemed he should easily have saved. In the 17th minute a back-pass from Kevin Hodges left Crudgington stranded and Caldwell whipped home his first. Russell Coughlin flared brief Argyle hopes of a fight-back with a Brazilian style 20-yard free-kick, but their defence boobed again just on half-time.

Adrian Burrows was dispossessed and a quick pass by Warren Joyce sent George Oghani in for his fifth goal of the season. Ten minutes into the second half Caldwell made it 4-1 with a cheeky lob over the goalkeeper and in the 61st minute Chandler converted a penalty after Gordon Nisbet had handled.

As Bolton caught their breath, Argyle got another consolation goal with a close-range header in the 69th minute from Tommy Tynan before 'keeper Crudgington damaged his hand. He was pushed upfield as a makeshift centre-forward with Nisbet taking over in goal.

One of the finest goals to be seen at Burnden that season came two minutes from time and took the Wanderers tally to the half-dozen. Oghani, latching on to a Caldwell pass, set off on a spell-binding dribble that took him through the entire Plymouth defence.

Oghani just couldn't manage to finish the job off himself. That was left to the ever alert Caldwell who slid in to complete a fine hat-trick.

Seconds later Oghani set off again.

Tony Caldwell slides in to make up the half-dozen and complete his hat-trick.

This time he settled for slipping the ball back for Chandler whose 25-yard angled shot seemed to go right through the arms of the emergency 'keeper.

Bolton Wanderers: Farnworth; Burrows, Phillips, Joyce, McElhinney, Valentine, Thompson, Chandler, Oghani, Caldwell, Bell. Sub: Rudge.

Plymouth Argyle: Crudgington; Nisbet, Uzzell, Harrison, Goodyear, Burrows, Hodges, Cooper, Tynan, Staniforth, Coughlin. Sub: Rogers for Harrison.

Attendance: 3,876
Referee: A.Saunders
(Newcastle upon Tyne)

We're All Going to Wemberlee...
9 May 1986
BOLTON WANDERERS 2 WIGAN ATHLETIC 1

The Wanderers put themselves 90 minutes away from their first Wembley appearance since 1958 when a last-minute Tony Caldwell goal gave them a 1-0 win at Springfield Park in the first leg of the Freight/Rover Trophy Northern Final.

Now, an atmosphere not seen at Burnden for many years saw a crowd of 12,120 get behind Bolton right from the start of the second leg against a side that had just missed out on promotion and hadn't lost away from home since December.

The team came on to the pitch to a ticker-tape reception with bags full of shredded paper being emptied into the Friday night air.

Unfortunately for the Wanderers things began badly. Wigan levelled the aggregate score inside the opening nine minutes when Paul Jewell capitalised on Steve Thompson's defensive error to thump the ball past Dave Felgate from a tight angle.

Bolton's pressurised defence managed to hold out to get some breathing space at the interval.

It was a different story after the break. Player-manager Phil Neal got his defence on the front foot whilst George Oghani and Tony Caldwell got their attacking act together.

Mark Came unleashed Bolton's first genuine goal assault in the 54th minute with a 30-yard shot that Roy Tunks held in a flying save. Midway through the half, Wigan centre-half Colin Methven failed to clear a cross and the ball fell to Oghani, who jinked past Tunks to run on and fire into the net for the night's equaliser.

The ground became a cauldron of noise but when Mark Gavin missed a simple chance with ten minutes remaining, if the doubts had started to creep in, the crowd didn't show it.

There were two minutes left when the irrepressible Oghani wriggled free to aim a high centre beyond the reach of Tunks. Caldwell spun round to crash a shot into the net and from then on it was chants of "Wembley here we come". What had been a poor season in the League would finish on a high note with a visit to the famous old stadium to face fellow Third Division side Bristol City.

Bolton Wanderers: Felgate; Scott, Phillips, Sutton, Came, Thompson, Neal, Oghani, Caldwell, Hartford, Gavin. Sub: Bell.

Wigan Athletic: Tunks; Cribley, Knowles, Walsh, Beesley, Methven, Lowe, Barrow, Jewell, Langley, Griffiths. Sub: Schofield for Knowles.

Attendance: 12,120
Referee: N.Wilson (Morecambe)

Player-manager Phil Neal (left) and his players celebrate reaching Wembley.

Shots Send Trotters Down

17 May 1987
BOLTON WANDERERS 2 ALDERSHOT 2

It was a black Sunday afternoon for the Wanderers. The players, trailing 1-0 from the first leg of the League Division Three-Four Play-off semi-final at The Recreation Ground, failed to make the most of home advantage even after two goals from Tony Caldwell took the game into extra-time.

They ended the season with a disastrous run of only two wins in 19 games, during which only nine goals were scored. Sections of supporters, understandably angry and frustrated by the club's slide from Division One to Division Four in only seven years, demonstrated inside the ground and again outside at the end.

The brand new Play-off system offered an escape route for the Wanderers who had finished fourth from bottom of the Third Division, well clear of the three automatic relegation places, but four points adrift of saving themselves from the Play-offs.

A heavy pitch wasn't conducive to attractive football but no one cared – all that mattered was the result. The breakthrough for Bolton came five minutes after the interval. Wanderers

broke out after surviving a defensive scare. Colin Smith's desperate tackle, sent Mark Gavin flying and Tony Caldwell managed to compose himself to convert the penalty.

It was Caldwell's first goal since the previous February and it lifted some of the tension but the Wanderers had 'keeper Dave Felgate to thank for some exciting saves. This was despite the fact that he was carrying a foot injury sustained during the first half. Aldershot kept plugging away and went ahead on aggregate in the 75th minute. Substitute Darren Anderson was first to react to a free-kick by Steven Wignall and the visitors had

144

the massive psychological advantage of an away goal.

Bolton had to score again to at least give themselves extra-time in which to secure a two-goal cushion and, with nine minutes remaining, Caldwell swooped to fire past Tony Lange to earn that opportunity. Extra-time was akin to suffering a slow death. Glenn Burvill scored Aldershot's second goal 13 minutes into the first period and it became obvious there was to be no way back.

Aldershot went on to defeat Wolves and win promotion to Division Three. The Wanderers, one of the Football League's founder members, would spend the League's centenary season in the Fourth Division for the first time. Depression reigned.

Bolton Wanderers: Felgate; Neal, Scott, Joyce, Sutton, Came, Caldwell, Thompson, Elliott, Hartford, Gavin. Sub: Stevens for Joyce.
Aldershot: Lange; Blankley, Friar, Fielder, Smith, Wignall, Mazzon, Burvill, Langley, McDonald, Johnson. Sub: Anderson for Langley.

Attendance: 7,445
Referee: B.T.Stephens (Stonehouse)

JT Goal Machine
28 November 1987
BOLTON WANDERERS 2 CAMBRIDGE UNITED 2

Bolton made a steady start to their first-ever Fourth Division term that had seen them placed just outside the top four. Unfortunately a number of clubs had already returned from Burnden with points under their belts – a situation that needed rectifying if promotion was to be won at the first attempt. Thirty-six-year-old player-manager Phil Neal stepped back into the Bolton defence for his first full game of the season.

Cambridge United were one of the best travelling sides in the League and they rose to their Burnden visit by taking an 18th-minute lead. Somehow, the smallest player on the Park, Peter Butler, got between Mark Came and Dean Crombie, to head home a cross by Gary Poole.

John Thomas, in his second spell at Burnden, had grabbed a dozen goals and increased his tally with a 31st-minute equaliser when Crombie and Steve Elliott combined to put Robbie Savage away to plant a perfect centre on to the head of the club's leading goalgetter.

Cambridge kept their heads but they had 'keeper Keith Branagan to thank for some safe handling. Later to come to Bolton Wanderers, Branagan was valued at £100,000 and was being watched by West Ham and Sunderland.

Reflex saves from Nicky Brookman's deflected shot and headers from Came and Trevor Morgan suggested he wouldn't be at the Abbey Stadium too long. Julian Darby hit both the bar and the post before Bolton went ahead in the 65th minute.

Thomas latched on to a Steve

John Thomas is denied by United goalkeeper Keith Branagan – who was to join Bolton for a later promotion campaign.

The Wanderers made good progress and got out of the Fourth Division at the first attempt. Against Cambridge United, John Thomas twice found the net.

Thompson pass and turned Poole only to be brought down by the full-back. Thomas got up to strike the penalty-kick confidently past Branagan for his seventh goal in five games.

Wanderers 'keeper Dave Felgate deprived United's attacking duo of John Purdie and Ian Benjamin but was helpless as they struck back to make it 2-2 in the 71st minute. John Beck's corner fell for Purdie to equalise, the Wanderers' defence clearly missing injured captain Dave Sutton.

The stage was then set for a grandstand finish but both sides had to settle for a point. This game echoed Bolton's season in many respects –

plenty of ups and downs, but a work rate that gave them the edge and most importantly of all, a regular goalgetter in John Thomas that would, in the end, earn promotion.

Bolton Wanderers: Felgate; Scott, Crombie, Savage, Came, Neal, Brookman, Thompson, Thomas, Elliott, Darby. Subs: Stevens, Morgan for Neal.
Cambridge United: Branagan; Poole, Murray, Smith, Crowe, Beck, Butler, Turner, Purdie, Benjamin, Kimble. Subs: Horwood, Beattie.

Attendance: 4,294
Referee: P.Vanes (Warley)

Winstanley Whips Wrexham
21 February 1989
BOLTON WANDERERS 3 WREXHAM 1 (AFTER EXTRA-TIME)

If ever there was a turning point to a Bolton season then this victory in the Sherpa Van Trophy Northern quarter-final can be said to have turned 1988-89.

With Bolton lying in Third Division

relegation trouble, the Sherpa Van Trophy provided some much needed distraction from League problems. Having come through the qualifying rounds the Wanderers won 1-0 at

Preston to set up this tie against the Welsh Fourth Division promotion-chasing outfit.

Manager Phil Neal chose to play a sweeper system against Wrexham's pacy attack. The ever-versatile Julian Darby dropped back into defence to partner Mark Winstanley and Dean Crombie came into the side to become the sweeper. Striker Mike Jeffrey made his full debut, replacing John Thomas who was struggling to find his form of the previous season.

Jeffrey showed plenty of promise and missed out on the only clear scoring chance of a dull first half when ex-Wanderer Mike Salmon saved his shot. Things warmed up after the interval – but only for Wrexham – Joey Jones converting Kevin Russell's 63rd-minute cross to put them in front.

Bolton seemed to be down and out, but a slice of luck and a spectacular goal changed everything. First, the referee waved away Wrexham's penalty appeals when Darby had clearly blocked Graham Cooper's header with his arm. Then in the 74th minute the Wanderers equalised from a most unlikely source.

Picking the ball up 40 yards from goal, Mark Winstanley let fly with a left-foot thunderbolt that left Salmon helpless.

Burnden was suddenly awake thanks to the stunning shot and the Wanderers stepped up a gear. Salmon had to be alert to save shots from Robbie Savage and Phil Brown to deny Wanderers a winner in normal time.

Seconds from the end of 90 minutes, Wrexham were reduced to ten men, Roger Preece being sent off for a second bookable offence.

Everyone was now looking forward to extra-time. That man Winstanley again popped up, scoring twice in a game for the first time in his career by heading Bolton's second eight minutes into extra-time from a corner by Savage.

Savage himself then put the issue beyond doubt with a low shot seven minutes later as confidence began to grow.

After this game, Bolton were unlucky to lose 1-0 at eventual champions Wolves, but then remained unbeaten until the end of the season, finishing in a comfortable tenth spot and going on

to win the Sherpa Van Trophy at Wembley – a run of 20 games.

Bolton Wanderers: Felgate; Brown, Cowdrill, Savage, Crombie, Winstanley, Storer, Thompson, Morgan, Jeffrey, Darby. Subs: Thomas for Storer, Henshaw.

Wrexham: Salmon; Salathiel, Wright, Hunter, Williams, Jones, Preece, Flynn, Cooper, Russell, Bowden. Subs. Thackeray for Flynn, Carter for Cooper.

Attendance: 3,833
Referee: D.Phillips (Barnsley)

Winstanley is on target again, this time heading his side ahead in extra-time.

21-year Jinx Ended
30 December 1989
BOLTON WANDERERS 3 BURY 1

Burnden Park's biggest League attendance for six years saw out the decade against local rivals Bury in this Third Division match, and witnessed a Wanderers League win over the Shakers for the first time in 21 years.

The jinx was ended in breathtaking style in what was an exciting clash between two closely-matched teams who were both in the promotion race. The Wanderers win sent them leapfrogging over Bury into fourth place.

After a run of six League games without a win, Bolton had got back into gear with a Burnden double over the Christmas holidays, commencing with a 2-0 win over Blackpool. The points earned against Bury confirmed that they were back in the hunt.

Bury, however, opened the better with winger David Lee's quicksilver raids causing problems in the Bolton defence. Phil Brown had to clear off his own line and the visitors could have been two up before Bolton's first serious attack of the afternoon.

Two goals in as many minutes then set the Wanderers on their way. Julian Darby's header from a Barry Cowdrill corner was forced home by David Reeves for him to record his first goal in over two months. Martin Pike, on loan from Sheffield United, set up the second when his free-kick was headed on by Stuart Storer for Reeves to send a powerful shot past Gary Kelly in the Bury goal.

Kelly then kept Bury in the game, denying Reeves a hat-trick and stopping a Tony Philliskirk close-range header. The visitors slowly regained the initiative and were rewarded in the 34th minute. Tony Cunningham's physical presence was decisive when he set up Liam Robinson to head beyond Dave Felgate.

One of the mainsprings of the Bolton attack was Barry Cowdrill who had been recalled to play on the left-hand side of midfield. He had a 54th-minute strike ruled out by a linesman's flag and there were plenty of nail-biting moments for both sides until the issue was put beyond doubt two minutes from time.

Stuart Storer stole in on the left to register his first League goal of the

season by heading in Philliskirk's cross.

The Wanderers managed to reach the Play-offs at the end of the season, despite a run of five League games without as much as a goal during March, but it proved to be too little too late as they went down 3-1 on aggregate to Notts County.

Bolton Wanderers: Felgate; Brown, Pike, Cowdrill, Crombie, Winstanley, Storer, Thompson, Reeves, Philliskirk, Darby. Subs: Came, Comstive.
Bury: Kelly; Hill, Withe, Hoyland, Clements, Knill, Lee, Robinson, Cunningham, Feeley, Bishop. Subs: Hulme for Withe, Parkinson.
Attendance: 10,628
Referee: G.Ashby (Worcester)

Stuart Storer heads Bolton's last goal of the 1980s as Bury are beaten.

Philliskirk's Play-off Pointer
22 May 1991
BOLTON WANDERERS 1 BURY 0

Wanderers manager Phil Neal hid his disappointment at reaching 83 points and not gaining one of the three automatic promotion places. After taking only seven points from the opening eight games, the Wanderers found themselves next to the bottom of the Division. A 2-2 draw at Bury on 13 October 1990 then set Bolton off on an undefeated run of 23 League games which put them firmly in the promotion race.

Unfortunately after that magnificent run there were slip-ups, including Bury's 3-1 win at Burnden, courtesy of a John McGinlay hat-trick. Four wins

Tony Philliskirk fires home the Play-off winner against Bury to get the Wanderers to Wembley.

and a draw in the final five League games were not enough, however, to pip Grimsby for third spot – the Mariners having a better goal-difference. Unlike the previous season the Wanderers went into the Play-offs full of confidence and, more importantly, in form. A 1-1 draw resulted in the first leg of the Division Three Play-off semi-final at Gigg Lane, both goals coming from penalties, David Lee scoring for Bury and Tony Philliskirk for Wanderers.

A crowd of 19,198 – the best at Burnden for ten years, saw Tony Philliskirk's late first-half goal clinch a nerve-racking victory in this second-leg match for Bolton to put them only 90 minutes away from promotion. In a close first half, Philliskirk notched his 28th goal of the season in time added on by the referee. Bury only managed to half clear Paul Comstive's corner and Julian Darby poked the ball forward to Philliskirk, who got in his left-foot shot that ended up in the back of the net.

The second half saw Bury getting on top, although not through their normal route. Winger David Lee was kept quiet by Barry Cowdrill and the Shakers had to rely on Charlie Bishop and Phil

Parkinson for inspiration. Dave Felgate made a number of vital saves, notably from Colin Greenall and Liam Robinson, as Bolton held on to their slender advantage. As the final whistle went the crowd invaded the pitch to celebrate reaching Wembley whilst Phil Neal wiped away tears of joy.

No one was to know at the time, but this game appeared to leave Bolton both mentally and physically drained. In the Play-off Final against Tranmere, Wanderers failed to reproduce their best form and went down 1-0 to an extra-time goal scored by Chris Malkin. After 49 games Bolton failed to gain promotion behind a side that had finished the season five points behind them in the final League table.

Bolton Wanderers: Felgate; Brown, Cowdrill, Comstive, Seagraves, Stubbs, Storer, Thompson, Philliskirk, Cunningham, Darby. Subs: Reeves, Green.

Bury: Kelly; Bishop, Stanislaus, Robinson, Valentine, Greenall, Lee, Sheron, Hulme, Parkinson, Kearney. Subs: Mauge, Atkin.

Attendance: 19,198
Referee: D.R.Elleray (Harrow)

Subs Stun Saints in Cup
16 February 1992
BOLTON WANDERERS 2 SOUTHAMPTON 2

Although Bolton were finding things difficult in the League, Burnden Park was one again buzzing with Cup fever and the arrival from Celtic of Andy Walker, who had scored in five of his first six games for the club.

The Wanderers had reached the fifth-round of the FA Cup for the first time since 1980 and were paired to meet the winners of the Manchester United-Southampton tie. The sides had drawn at The Dell and the Saints produced a Cup shock by winning the replay on penalties at Old Trafford.

Bolton had already produced something of a shock themselves having accounted for Second Division Brighton & Hove Albion in the previous round at Burnden.

Before a virtual sell-out crowd, the Wanderers made a good start, Julian Darby forcing 'keeper Tim Flowers into a save and Tony Philliskirk having an effort ruled out for offside.

Things changed in the 26th minute when the First Division side went ahead. Richard Hall was given too much room and he headed the Saints in front from a Matthew Le Tissier corner.

Three minutes later, in a carbon-copy move, Hall looked to have killed the tie with his second goal as Bolton's defence crumbled. The crowd went silent as Bolton looked for a way back but without much joy. Former Bury winger David Lee hit the net for Southampton only to be ruled offside but it looked as though Wanderers' record of never having lost a game on a Sunday was about to go.

The introduction of David Reeves on the hour improved matters as his direct running began to make some impression on the visitors' defence. In the 78th minute, manager Phil Neal made his second substitution, bringing on Scott Green, who had been dropped from the starting line up to make way for Michael Brown.

Within a minute he was involved in setting up Bolton's first goal, Andy Walker sweeping a left-foot volley past Flowers to set up an unbelievable finish. The Burnden roar returned and Southampton began to wobble as the Wanderers made wave after wave of attacks.

Four minutes from time the equaliser came, Green netting Reeves' cross at full reach with a header that was greeted with both joy and relief by the Bolton faithful.

The Wanderers were not worried by a replay and at The Dell were seconds

Top: Andy Walker sweeps home the Wanderers' first goal past Southampton's Tim Flowers.
Middle: Scott Green heads the equaliser against the Saints.
Bottom: The Burnden side celebrate the goal which capped a great Cup performance.

from reaching the sixth round before Barry Horne hit a 35-yard equaliser to make it 2-2 in injury time. Southampton finally won 3-2 in extra-time, leaving Bolton with only the satisfaction of being the last Third Division side in that season's competition.

Bolton Wanderers: Felgate; Spooner, Burke, Kelly, Seagraves, Came, Brown, Patterson, Walker, Philliskirk, Darby, Subs: Reeves for Patterson, Green for Brown.

Southampton: Flowers; Kenna, Adams, Horne, Hall, Ruddock, Le Tissier, Cockerill, Shearer, Gray, Benali. Subs: Dowie, Lee for Adams.

Attendance: 20,136
Referee: M.Peck (Kendal)

Trotters Turn on the Heat
3 January 1993
BOLTON WANDERERS 2 LIVERPOOL 2

If the Wanderers had staged their own version of the great escape in the FA Cup 12 months earlier against Southampton, then it was Liverpool's turn in this high noon Sunday third-round encounter.

After a slow start to the season, Bruce Rioch's side had climbed into a top-six place by the end of 1992 and were unbeaten in ten League games.

In bitterly cold conditions, the Wanderers went ahead after only seven minutes when the sure-footed John McGinlay collected Scott Green's low angled ball to go around Mike Hooper and slot home.

McGinlay then forced a mix up between Hooper and Torben Piechnik only to see his shot strike a post. The rebound fell to David Lee who saw his effort go over the bar, but frustration was forgotten as Mark Seagraves headed home Mark Patterson's corner in the 22nd minute and for a while it looked as if the Wanderers would finish the tie before half-time.

Andy Walker twice went close to increasing the lead in what was 45 minutes of sheer enjoyment for Bolton supporters.

Liverpool came back, as expected, after the interval but the Premier League side had Lady Luck to thank for getting something from it. A ricochet from a block tackle by McGinlay on the halfway line in the

56th minute sent substitute Ronnie Rosenthal clear. He struck the post with his shot but the rebound came back into the path of Mark Winstanley who couldn't get out of the way and the ball ended up in the back of the net.

There were only seven minutes left when a miscued back pass by Seagraves was capitalised on by Steve McManaman. His effort was blocked by Keith Branagan but the rebound fell kindly to Ian Rush who hit his 39th FA Cup goal to earn the FA Cup holders a replay.

The Liverpool press suggested that after coming so close to defeat, the Anfield side might have what it takes to make another Wembley trip – but the Wanderers proved otherwise.

In the replay the Wanderers were lifted by a start even better than the one enjoyed at Burnden. It took only three minutes for John McGinlay to rise to head home David Lee's left-wing cross. Bolton's dominance of the first half was marginal in comparison to the first game but nevertheless they should have led by a bigger margin at the interval.

Bolton looked dangerous several times as the match drew to a tense finale, notably when Scott Green and Andy Walker hurried their shots when they had more time than they realised. But it was no more than they deserved when Walker found yards of space at the far post to convert McGinlay's

right-wing cross 11 minutes from time to put 9,000 Bolton fans into ecstasy.

Bolton Wanderers: Branagan; Brown, Burke, Lee, Seagraves, Winstanley, Green, Kelly, Walker, McGinlay, Patterson. Subs: McAteer, Stubbs.

Liverpool: Hooper; Marsh, Jones, Nicol, Piechnik, Bjørnebye, McManaman, Hutchinson, Rush, Barnes, Thomas. Subs: Rosenthal for Thomas, Stewart.

Attendance: 21,502
Referee: R.Groves (Weston-super-Mare)

Scottish Duo Stun Stockport

6 April 1993

BOLTON WANDERERS 2 STOCKPORT COUNTY 1

This Burnden Park Division Two promotion showdown with Stockport County brought together two of the League's most prolific goalscorers. Andy Walker – the bargain buy from Glasgow Celtic 15 months earlier – had scored 31 goals in 42 Wanderers appearances so far that season, whilst Kevin Francis – the Football League's tallest player at 6ft 7in – had grabbed 34 goals in 49 Stockport games.

The Wanderers were locked together with Stockport and West Brom on 66 points, six behind second-placed Port

Andy Walker heads Bolton into an early lead against Stockport County.

Vale, and both were in form. Bolton were unbeaten in ten League outings, the last defeat being against Stockport at Edgeley Park on 9 February, whilst County were undefeated in five games.

The game was also to be a contrast in styles and it was Bolton's slick passing that got them off to a flying start. Only two minutes had gone when John McGinlay latched on to a poor clearance by County defender Tony Barrass. The Scot sent David Lee racing away down the right wing to deliver a delightful cross that Walker nodded past stranded 'keeper Phil Kite.

This took Walker's goal tally to 50 for the club and there was to be another half-century celebration five minutes after the interval. Once again it was Lee, who caused umpteen problems for the visitors' defence, that got in a telling cross and this time John McGinlay rose above everyone to put Bolton two up. This took the Wanderers' Scottish striking partnership to 50 for the term.

For a spell the Wanderers dominated and another goal would have put the issue beyond any doubt. County, however, capitalised on a mix-up between Jason McAteer and Tony Kelly in the 63rd minute, Martin James crossing to find the head of Kevin Francis to give him his 35th goal of the season and a share of Stockport's post war scoring record held by Jack Connor.

The pressure was intense in the final stages as Stockport piled forward but the centre-back pairing of Mark Seagraves and Alan Stubbs made sure there were no more defensive slip-ups. Indeed, it was Walker who came closest to scoring for the Wanderers, a spectacular volley rattling the crossbar.

It proved to be a more than successful night for Bolton, who learned after the game that Port Vale, who were being chased for the second automatic promotion place, had slipped up at home by drawing 2-2 with relegation-threatened Preston North End.

John McGinlay makes it two against Stockport and Bolton are nearer still to promotion.

John McGinlay converts a penalty against Preston in the final game of the season that earns promotion to Division One.

Sadly for Andy Walker, he was to play only two more games before suffering an injury that would keep him out of the game for nine months. The season went to the wire and Bolton, who had been in the bottom four after 12 games, earned runners-up spot to Stoke City on the final day with a 1-0 win over Preston at Burnden. The largest crowd of the season, 21,720 seeing a 74th-minute John McGinlay penalty send Preston into Division Three and condemn Port Vale to the Play-offs.

Bolton Wanderers: Branagan; Brown, Burke, Lee, Seagraves, Stubbs, Kelly, McAteer, Walker, McGinlay, Green. Subs: Winstanley, Parkinson for Green.
Stockport County: Kite; Flynn, P.R.Williams, Frain, Miller, Barrass, Gannon, Ward, Francis, Beaumont, James. Subs: Todd for Frain, P.A.Williams for Barrass.
Attendance: 13,733
Referee: V.Callow (Solihull)

He Gets the Ball, He Scores a Goal, Owen Coyle
13 November 1993
GRETNA 2 BOLTON WANDERERS 3

If ever there was a sense of relief of getting out of jail in a game at Burnden Park, then this FA Cup first-round tie was it. Scottish side Gretna, from the Northern Premier League First Division, switched the tie from their Raydale Park ground where the capacity was a mere 1,900.

The Wanderers who as the 'away' side changed from their normal colours, were in at the first round despite winning promotion to the First Division the previous season and were facing non-League opposition, at this stage of the FA Cup competition, for the fourth consecutive season.

Since the formation of the Football League in 1888, Bolton had faced non-League opposition on 35 occasions, losing only six times, the last being at Burnden in season 1910-11 at the hands of Midland League Chesterfield.

However, only 11 minutes had gone when the Scottish Borders club went ahead. Wanderers failed to clear a free-kick and tall centre-half Derek Townsley stole in to rattle the ball into the net. This didn't seem to worry the crowd – they seemed pleased to see the non-Leaguers make a game of it.

Two minutes later Owen Coyle was blatantly pushed inside the penalty area and John McGinlay stepped up to convert his kick for an equaliser to settle any nerves.

Gretna, however, kept on plugging away and in the 25th minute again found the net with what was only their second attempt at goal. The Wanderers' defence again crumbled and Mark Dobie side-footed past Aidan Davison.

There was still no great panic as the Wanderers would surely come back to steal the tie – wouldn't they?

Seven minutes after the interval, former Celtic winger John Halpin got the better of full-back Phil Brown and was inches of getting a third for Gretna with a super chip shot. Slowly, however, Bolton began to get on top in midfield, but Gretna 'keeper Jason Priestley, a trainee policeman playing his first game of the season, performed heroics to inspire his defenders.

Even when he was beaten, as was the case in the 76th minute, the crossbar came to the rescue, Jason McAteer holding his head in his hands at the outcome of his effort.

Thoughts of what would have been the club's worst FA Cup defeat in its history evaporated in the 79th minute. McAteer again worked through the middle and this time the ball broke kindly for Coyle to side foot the equaliser.

The relief around Burnden was immense, Coyle's eye for goal had at last got the fans warming to him after a tough start to his Bolton career having joined the club from Airdrieonians.

The Scot then became not only the saviour, but the hero with what turned out to be Bolton's winner six minutes

Owen Coyle turns away after equalising against Gretna to save Bolton's blushes.

Coyle runs in to strike a late winner against the Scottish non-League side.

from time with a close-range header from David Lee's cross. Bolton were on another FA Cup journey that was to be full of shocks, good football and, above all, excitement.

Bolton Wanderers: Davison; Brown, Phillips, McAteer, Stubbs, Winstanley, Lee, Green, Coyle, McGinlay, Thompson. Subs: Kelly for Green, Seagraves, Hoult.

Gretna: Priestley, Armstrong, McCartney, Gorman, Gardiner, Townsley, Halpin, Walsh, Walker, Dobie, Potts. Subs: Monaghan for Walker, Ealing for Potts, Sweating.

Attendance: 6,447
Referee: E.Lomax (Manchester)

Arsenal 'Gunned' Down in FA Cup

31 January 1994
BOLTON WANDERERS 2 ARSENAL 2

Having escaped elimination by the skin of their teeth in the first round of the FA Cup at the hands of Gretna, the Wanderers went on to make more FA Cup headlines.

A win in the second round at Lincoln City was a professional performance, but the scalp of Premier League side Everton in the third round once again made the country's footballing public sit up and take notice. After a 1-1 draw at Burnden, Bolton then went to Goodison and came from a two goal deficit to win 3-2 in extra-time with Owen Coyle getting the winner. The Wanderers now had the chance of knocking the Cup holders out of the competition for the second season in succession, having accounted for Liverpool in 1993, the last club having achieved that feat being Chelsea in 1965.

The Sky TV cameras came to Burnden Park for this fourth-round tie hoping to witness another night of Cup fever and they certainly got their money's worth for entertainment value. Bolton dominated the opening half and went ahead in the 31st minute when John McGinlay put through an inch-perfect pass for Jason McAteer to shoot past David Seaman.

At the interval Wanderers were worthy of more than that slender lead but that disappeared six minutes into the second half. Paul Merson's right-wing cross took a deflection and Ian Wright was on hand to convert the easiest of chances for the Gunners equaliser.

Arsenal then began to hold the initiative and went ahead in the 66th minute when Tony Adams was allowed too much space to head in Nigel Winterburn's free-kick.

The Wanderers' 'never say die' attitude was again in evidence as they went all out to save the game. Fifteen minutes from time, Andy Walker was brought off the bench to make his return after his long-term injury, the cheers from the Burnden terraces raised the tempo.

There were only four minutes left on

the clock when Bolton got a deserved equaliser with what was the best goal of the game. Tony Kelly hit a superb left-sided cross that found McGinlay at the far post. The Scot headed firmly back across the face of goal for Owen Coyle to volley into the roof of the net to keep up his record of having scored in every round.

That equaliser gave the Wanderers yet another visit to a top Premiership club and Highbury certainly wasn't going to hold any fears for them. The 4,500 Bolton supporters created a *mardi gras* atmosphere at the Clock End of the ground – out-singing and out-cheering the home supporters.

John McGinlay headed his 21st goal of the season after 20 minutes and this gave Bolton the momentum to earn victory despite conceding a 35th-minute equaliser to Alan Smith.

The Wanderers defended intelligently and counter-attacked with speed and purpose but needed extra-time to secure progress. Owen Coyle struck the upright and Jason McAteer fired home the rebound, Andy Walker fired low under David Seaman and Arsenal were

'lucky' it was only 3-1. In the dying minutes Tony Kelly had what appeared to be a perfectly good goal ruled out and the Londoners, who went on to win the European Cup-winners Cup, were reduced to ten men when Martin Keown was sent off for a second bookable offence.

Eventual Coca-Cola Cup winners Aston Villa were accounted for in the next round as Bolton reached the FA Cup quarter-finals for the first time since 1959. Oldham Athletic ended the adventure with a 1-0 win at Burnden – but it had been sweet.

Bolton Wanderers: Davison; Brown, Phillips, Kelly, McAteer, Winstanley, Lee, Stubbs, Coyle, McGinlay, Patterson. Subs: Walker for Patterson, Burke, Hoult.
Arsenal: Seaman; Dixon, Winterburn, Hillier, Bould, Adams, Keown, Parlour, Merson, Campbell, Wright. Subs: Smith for Parlour, Jensen, Miller.

Attendance: 18,891
Referee: T.Holbrook (Wolverhampton). Substituted at half-time by B.Preist (Halesowen).

1994-95 – Burnden Park's Dramatic Centenary Season

BURNDEN Park's 100th year was as dramatic as any seen in the ground's illustrious history.

Not only did Bolton Wanderers defeat two Premier League sides before their own supporters, to reach the League Cup Final (Coca Cola Cup) for

the first time, but only one First Division reverse was incurred, form that was to catapult the club into the drama of the Play-offs.

The season began with a visit by Liverpool for a friendly, which was won 4-1 by the Trotters. It was a fixture

The Birdman of Burnden Park

During Bolton's FA Cup fourth-round game against Arsenal at Burnden on Monday, 31 January 1994, which was televised live on Sky TV, play was suspended at a crucial stage when the attention of the whole stadium turned skywards. Both the players

and crowd saw someone buzz the top of the stadium from a fan-powered parachute. The game was in its 29th minute when the incident took place and thankfully the 'birdman' disappeared to allow the play to continue.

repeated the following April at Wembley Stadium, although this time, unfortunately, the result was different. The Premier League side won 2-1 but Bolton did, however, have the satisfaction of taking part in a tremendous game that saw a superb goal by the Trotters' Alan Thompson.

Bristol City capitalised on the Wanderers' notorious slow start and won the opening League fixture at Burnden by 2-0. The Wanderers then remained unbeaten on home soil. A run of 26 League and Cup games that saw a rise from the previous season's average League attendance of 10,498 to 13,029. This was due, not only to results, but also to an entertaining brand of football instigated by the management team of Bruce Rioch and Colin Todd.

Having produced some memorable performances in the previous season's FA Cup, in 1994-95 the Wanderers saw a similar trend, only this time in the League Cup. A Richard Sneekes goal at Burnden completed a 4-0 aggregate success over Ipswich early in the season, whilst a fifth-round tie against Norwich saw possibly the best goal and best save of the season.

David Lee's 66th-minute winner was something special: skipping past three defenders in a 30-yard run he released

an unstoppable shot. At the other end, Keith Branagan produced an acrobatic save from an injury-time free-kick by Ian Crook and Bolton thus earned a semi-final place in the competition for only the second time.

First Division strugglers Swindon Town were the opposition but they were to be the most difficult team to overcome during the cup run. Bolton reached Wembley the hard way, after losing 2-1 in the first leg at the County Ground, they found themselves a goal down at Burnden. Everything changed in the 61st minute with the introduction of both Mixu Paatelainen and Richard Sneekes.

Three minutes later Alan Thompson hit the bar and Jason McAteer was on hand to force home the rebound. In the 70th minute Paatelainen levelled the aggregate scores with a ferocious drive and with only two minutes left to play John McGinlay hit the winner. The game produced the ground's record gate receipts of £159,290.50.

Only 13 League goals were conceded at 'fortress' Burnden during the season. This total has only once been bettered by the club, that being in 1972-73 when only nine were conceded as the Third Division championship was secured. Grimsby Town were the only club to

score three goals at Burnden when, just before Christmas, Bolton found themselves two down early on. They hit back to lead 3-2 but a late equaliser meant a share of the spoils.

This wasn't to be the only six goal thriller at Burnden during 1994-95. In January, Charlton Athletic were defeated 5-1 and the following month promotion rivals Wolverhampton Wanderers suffered the same fate.

In the final analysis it was the Wanderers away from that was to cost the club any chance of the championship. Rivals, Middlesbrough, who were eventual champions, Reading, Wolves, Tranmere Rovers and Barnsley were all defeated at Burnden. However the Wanderers didn't manage to earn as much as a point from their return visits.

And so after being in the promotion frame for most of the season, Bolton had to settle for third spot and a place in the Play-offs against Wolverhampton Wanderers.

Above: John McGinlay and Jason McAteer celebrate after the Scot had hit the winner against Swindon Town in the Coca Cola Cup semi-final.

Below: The Burnden groundstaff clear the covers that helped the 1994-95 game against Charlton to go ahead.

Players dejected after the 2-1 Coca Cola Cup Final defeat by Liverpool.

John McGinlay sets Burnden alight with his opener against Wolves in the Play-off semi-final.

In a 2-1 reverse at Molineux, a Jason McAteer strike gave the Wanderers a precious away goal to bring back to Burnden. Three days later Wolves visited, looking to gain revenge for their heavy League defeat, against a Bolton side depleted through injury and suspension. Burnden's best crowd of the season, 20,041, produced an atmosphere reminiscent of the 1970s promotion winning seasons and played

their part as Bolton overturned the deficit to win 2-0 and 3-2 on aggregate after extra-time.

John McGinlay levelled the aggregate scores just before half-time and hit the winner five minutes into the second period of extra-time. Even then, Bolton did it the hard way, having lost influential players David Lee and Alan Stubbs during the game through injury.

Having kept their supporters on

Top: Mixu
Paatelainen,
Fabian
DeFreitas and
Owen Coyle
celebrate
victory at
Wembley.

Left: Scott
Green, John
McGinlay and
Keith
Branagan after
the sensational
Play-off Final
against
Reading.

tenterhooks in the semi-finals, the Wanderers then went one better by sending them on an emotional roller-coaster in the Play-off Final against Reading at Wembley.

Two goals ahead inside 12 minutes, Reading appeared to be ending a 124-year wait to join football's top league when they had the opportunity to make it three after winning a penalty kick in the 35th minute. Goalkeeper Keith Branagan saved Stuart Lovell's effort and from that moment on the pendulum began to swing slowly towards the Trotters.

Fifteen minutes from time Owen

Bruce Rioch (left) and Colin Todd, the men who steered the Wanderers into the Premier League. A few days after the Wembley victory, Rioch took over as manager of Arsenal, the lure of a world-famous club and the fact that his family live near London were too great to resist.

Coyle pulled one back and with only four minutes left on the clock, Fabian DeFreitas levelled the scores to force extra-time. The Wanderers and their supporters had now recovered and were building up to a grand finale that saw Mixu Paatelainen and DeFreitas again hit the back of the net. Reading's player-manager Jimmy Quinn hit a last minute consolation to make it 4-3.

Burnden Park can now celebrate its centenary with the Wanderers in the same company as when it opened in 1895, in football's élite.

Bolton Wanderers celebrate promotion on the steps of Bolton Town Hall after defeating Reading at Wembley.

Bring on the Substitute!

Burnden Park made history on 21 August 1965, the opening day of the 1965-66 season, when the first-ever substitute in the Football League was used.

Charlton Athletic were the visitors for a Second Division fixture and they lost goalkeeper Michael Rose early on through injury. Former Scottish international full-back John Hewie took over in goal and Keith Peacock came on as substitute.

Peacock went on to make 533 League appearances for Charlton, his only League club, in a career that spanned 1962 to 1978. Bolton won 4-2 that day, thanks to two goals from Francis Lee, one of which came from the penalty spot, on-form Warwick Rimmer and an own-goal by Billy Bonds. Len Glover and Roy Matthews scored for Charlton.

John Hulme was the Trotters' 12th man that day but wasn't called upon. Bolton's first substitution came on the 9 October 1965 when Gordon Taylor replaced the injured John Napier in a 3-2 defeat by Southampton at Burnden Park.

Taylor was also Bolton's first goalscoring substitute but that wasn't until September 1969. Then he came on for John Ritson in a 2-0 defeat of Birmingham City at Burnden.

Two substitutes were first allowed in season 1987-88. Wigan Athletic were the first side to use both at Burnden during their 3-1 Littlewoods Cup first-round, second-leg tie on 25 August 1987, Mark Hilditch and Ian Griffiths replacing Stuart Storer (who later signed for Bolton) and Paul Cook.

The Wanderers first used both substitutes in a 2-1 defeat at Torquay on 19 September 1987 and a week later again used both in an identical result against Hartlepool United at Burnden. Then Steve Elliott and player-manager Phil Neal replaced Trevor Morgan and Julian Darby.

Aidan Davison was Bolton's first substitute goalkeeper after the introduction of three

Gordon Taylor, Bolton's first substitute to appear when he came on in October 1965.

substitutes in 1993-94 season. He replaced Keith Branagan who suffered cruciate ligament damage during a 2-0 reverse against Derby County at Burnden in October 1993. Curiously, in the previous home game against Millwall, Davison played after Branagan was injured in the warm-up and had to revert to the bench.

Testimonials at Burnden Park

In the early days of League football, the Wanderers would take part in other friendly matches on opponents' grounds in aid of players who had suffered injury. These, however, became too frequent and found no place in the modern game without just cause.

Indeed, the first game on Burnden itself was a benefit for Wanderers' full-back and captain Di Jones, who had served the club for seven seasons. Twelve months later, in September 1896, international goalkeeper John Sutcliffe was the next recipient, Bolton defeating Bury 4-0 at Burnden.

Benefit games were later extended to cover League encounters with players receiving their cheque from the match takings. During

the 1920s these became quite common with such great players as Joe Smith and Dick Pym earning due recognition for service in this way.

The rules were later changed to prevent these sort of payments for what, in some cases, were only short periods of service. The modern game saw the disappearance of the benefit to be replaced by the testimonial. These were to be granted at the club's discretion to players who had suffered injury, and therefore livelihood, and to players who had seen at least ten years' service with one club.

The first of the modern day testimonials to take place at Burnden Park was in April 1957

George Taylor (far right), welcomes (left to right) Tom Finney, Nat Lofthouse and Sir Stanley Matthews to his testimonial game in April 1967.

when Bolton defeated an All Stars XI by 3-0 on behalf of Harold Hassall. His career had come to a premature end on New Year's Day 1955 when his right knee was shattered in a League game against Chelsea. A crowd of 20,000 saw Dennis Stevens get two goals, with the other coming from Doug Holden, who was one of Hassall's teammates in the 1953 FA Cup Final defeat against Blackpool.

It was injury that prompted the next testimonial game to be played on the ground on 16 October 1961. The Wanderers' greatest goalscorer, Nat Lofthouse, who netted 285 goals in 503 first-class appearances for the club was rewarded for his services with a Bolton 1958 XI against an All Star side.

Another of Bolton's greats was rewarded in April 1967 when the club saw fit to allow a Bolton XI take on an All Star side on behalf of George Taylor. His loyalty to the club was without question. Having served 21 seasons as a player, clocking up 546 games including wartime appearances, he added another 20 years as coach to the team which included the FA Cup winning side of 1958.

On 1 April 1969, Roy Hartle, who had been only one first-class appearance short of the 500 mark, staged his International XI against an All Star XI. It was a nostalgic return to Burnden Park for Francis Lee, who hit five goals for the All Star's who ran out 10-9 winners!

This was pure entertainment for the crowd of 8,478 who could turn their back on the Wanderers' relegation problems at that time. Indeed, six days later, Bristol City visited

Burnden for a Second Division fixture which attracted only 8,172.

The first 'real' international testimonial at Burnden was played on behalf of former England international goalkeeper Eddie Hopkinson. He had appeared in a club record 519 League games and had attracted Portuguese World Cup stars Eusébio and Simoes to take part for a European XI against his selected XI.

Only three days after Bolton had been relegated to the Third Division for the first time in their history, a crowd of 16,307, the best that season at Burnden, saw the European side win 6-4. As a prelude to the main match a Wanderers 1958 XI defeated an All Star side by 3-2.

Bolton Wanderers were involved in a testimonial at Burnden for the first time since 1957 in May 1973. The Wanderers had just won the Third Division championship and they took on Second Division championship winners Burnley on behalf of club captain Warwick Rimmer who had been at Burnden since 1958.

Both clubs paraded their silverware before the game which attracted 13,314. Bolton came from behind to win a competitive encounter by 3-1 with all their goals coming after the interval.

In May 1976 there was something of an anticlimax around the ground for Roy Greaves' testimonial. The Wanderers had just missed out on promotion to Division One and no doubt this restricted the crowd down to 6,000 for a game between Bolton and an

All Star XI who won 2-1.

In contrast, the next testimonial took place in May 1978, just after the Wanderers had won promotion, 20,516 paying to see Bolton draw 5-5 with a Liverpool-Everton select side. This game was on behalf of Peter Thompson, who had spent over ten years with Liverpool, but such was his influence on the revival of fortunes at Bolton that it was felt that the game should take place at his final club from where he had just retired.

Liverpool brought along the European Cup and fielded nine of the side that had won the trophy against Bruges. Bolton fielded the side that had clinched the title against Fulham with the exception of Peter Thompson taking over from Alan Gowling. Bolton paraded the Second Division championship trophy and in a carnival atmosphere the players produced a memorable evening. Even the goalkeepers got their chance to shine. Liverpool's Ray Clemence and the Wanderers' Jim McDonagh spent the second half playing up front for their sides, McDonagh even managing to get on to the score-sheet with the final goal of the evening.

In November 1978, former Burnden hero John Byrom returned to don a white shirt as the Wanderers faced Blackburn Rovers. Unfortunately only 2,000 turned up to see the visitors run out 4-3 winners, the Wanderers scoring three times in the final five minutes. Two of these were netted by Byrom's former striking partner Garry Jones in what was to be his last appearance for the club.

Peter Nicholson was the next former Trotter to be rewarded for ten years' service to the club. His game took place in October 1982 when the Wanderers took on a Bolton 1978 side that included Frank Worthington and George Best who guested.

The opponents for the last three testimonial games at Burnden have, on each

occasion, been Manchester City.

In August 1989 the Maine Road club ran out 2-0 winners before 8,783 in a game that was organised to commemorate the Golden Jubilee of Nat Lofthouse signing for the Wanderers and his 50 years service to the game.

In October 1990, the Wanderers defeated City 2-1 in a testimonial arranged for Freddie Hill. A crowd of 2,810 paid their tributes to a player that had represented both clubs as well as his country in a career that had spanned 510 League games.

The most recent testimonial to be staged on the ground was in November 1992 when the Wanderers defeated City 4-2 before a crowd of 2,152. This game was a joint testimonial for Frank Worthington and Robbie Savage who had retired from the game through injury whilst with the club.

The dwindling attendances merely reflected a general trend where friendly matches have become far less appealing with the growth of competitive football.

Ray Train and Jim McDonagh show off their Second Division championship medals after playing in Peter Thompson's testimonial in 1978.

The Oval-Shaped Ball Comes to Burnden Park

It was perhaps fitting that Swinton RL club were the first side to use Burnden for a game of rugby. Back in January 1893, the Wanderers had faced Blackburn Rovers in a friendly that had resulted in a 1-1 draw at Station Road, home of Swinton.

On Wednesday, 23 January 1985, the Lions took on Sheffield Eagles in a Rugby League Second Division fixture thanks to the Burnden pitch being frost free due to its undersoil heating. The game, however, began 20 minutes late after Sheffield's coach had broken down coming over the Pennines.

An untimely blizzard kept the attendance to half the anticipated figure but 1,438, close to Swinton's average for the season, saw them triumph by 14 points to 8.

The pitch was playing well despite the fact

that on the previous evening the Wanderers had defeated Crewe in the Freight/Rover Trophy and, three days later, Rotherham were beaten 2-0 in a League game.

On Sunday, 10 February 1985, Burnden again came to the rescue, this time to stage a first-round Silk Cut Challenge Cup-tie between Wigan and Batley. Wigan ran out 46-8 winners before a crowd of 9,606.

During 1985-86, Swinton used Burnden Park on three occasions. In August they entertained St Helens, and in March the Lions played a reserve fixture against the same opponents and a League game with Wigan.

The only Rugby League games played during 1986-87 came within eight days of one another during January. Firstly the Final of

the John Player Special Trophy between Wigan and Warrington attracted the ground's best gate for six years, 21,144. Only 1,169 spectators then saw Swinton defeat Huddersfield 48-10 in a Second Division game.

In 1987-88, Burnden hosted two semi-finals involving Wigan. In December, Leeds ran out 19-6 winners in the John Player Special Trophy before a 13,538 crowd which was a record for that stage of the competition. The following March, Wigan reached Wembley with an emphatic win over Salford in the Silk Cut Challenge Cup before a crowd of over 20,000. The Wanderers had switched their Fourth Division game against Darlington to the previous evening to

accommodate the semi-final.

The first RL Final to be held at Burnden came in January 1989 with Bolton again switching to Friday night to allow the ground to be used. Wigan were once again involved and they lifted the John Player Special Trophy by defeating Widnes 12-6.

On 23 March 1991, Wigan defeated Oldham 30-16 in the Silk Cut Challenge Cup semi-final to reach Wembley for a fourth consecutive season. Twelve months later Wigan did it again in what was the most recent RL game on the ground. This was the most one-sided Challenge Cup semi-final in the game's history with Bradford going down 71-10.

Burnden Park – Firsts, Lasts and Oddities

'Burnden' – Scottish terminology for a brook or stream is a burn. 'Den' comes from an old English word dene or denu meaning a valley. Thus in literal terms Burnden is a valley with a stream flowing through it. The particular stream was Burnden Brook which originally flowed from Rose Hill. Later culverted, it then ran underneath both the Manchester Road and the ground itself.

In the late 18th century, on the site of the ground, stood Burnden poor house which was a shelter for the paupers of the locality. During the 19th century a notorious body snatcher by the name of Hannah used the area as a store for his 'merchandise.'

The first reserve game to take place on the ground was on 28 September 1895 when Burnley were defeated 5-1 in a Lancashire Combination fixture. Jim Cassidy, who had lost his first-team place to Bob Jack after the opening four League fixtures, netted three goals to become the first player to get a hat-trick on the ground.

The first addition to the ground once it had opened was a reporters' box on the Manchester Road side. This was built to save messengers dashing all the way around the ground and was in action for the visit of Bury in October 1895.

Bury were the first club to win a Football League game at Burnden Park when on 5 October

1895 they ran out 4-2 winners. Earlier that season the Trotters had won 3-0 at Gigg Lane but they were to gain further revenge by knocking the Shakers out of the FA Cup in February 1896.

The first fatality on the ground occurred on 26 October 1895 during a League clash with Stoke. A spectator on the Embankment side of the arena had clambered on to the railway for a better view of the game. Unfortunately due to the loose cinders he slipped and fell between the buffers of two coal waggons, the engine slackened and he was crushed.

The first postponement at Burnden was on 16 November 1895 when Small Heath were due to play the Trotters in a Football League fixture. The pitch had failed its first test in not being able to take any water, the ground being six inches under in places due to the poor drainage. Indeed, inside four months, not only were the club having problems with the pitch but the cycling track was also beginning to break up due to the elements.

Some of the club's reserve fixtures were switched back to Pikes Lane, the surroundings there being bleak after the dismantling of the stand. The pitch at Burnden didn't improve quickly and there was another 'incident' on 28 December 1895.

Preston North End were the visitors for a League game and, after a scoreless first half, they refused to come out to continue for the second half, complaining about the state of the puddled pitch. The referee, Mr J.Lewis, had no option other than to abandon the game much, to the displeasure of the 2,000 crowd.

The first game to take place on a Christmas Day at Burnden was in 1895 when Liverpool visited for a friendly. The game ended scoreless.

On New Year's Day 1895, Bolton entertained their first ever crowd of 20,000 which produced then record receipts of £484. Derby County were the opponents, two goals from Jimmy Gunn earning Bolton a 2-1 win.

Three days later, on 4 January 1896, Billy Joyce, Wanderers' centre-forward was the first player to sustain serious injury on the ground. In scoring one of the goals that defeated Wolves 4-0 he broke his right leg and that kept him out of the game for over 12 months. Despite this he still ended season 1895-96 as the club's leading goalscorer with 12.

The first Cup-tie at Burnden was on 19 January 1896 when Bolton lost 2-1 to Burnley in the first round of the Lancashire Cup. Robert Tannahill was Bolton's scorer.

The first FA Cup-tie at Burnden attracted a crowd of 16,397. This took place on 29 February 1896 and the opponents were Bury. The Wanderers had got through the first two rounds with away victories at Crewe Alexandra and Blackpool. Jocky Wright and Jimmy Gunn scored Bolton's goals that defeated the Shakers 2-0 to send the Wanderers into the semi-finals where they went down to Sheffield Wednesday after a replay.

The first Cup Final to be staged at Burnden Park was the Lancashire Junior Cup Final on 21 March 1896. Blackburn Park Road, who the Wanderers had once beaten 10-4 in the Lancashire Cup at Pikes Lane, took the trophy with a 3-1 defeat of Skerton before 2,000 spectators.

Seven days later, on 28 March, Burnden Park was selected to host the Lancashire Cup Final, a crowd of 13,000 watching Bury and Blackburn Rovers draw 1-1. In the replay, also staged at Burnden on 18 April 1896, 17,597 saw Blackburn win the trophy by winning 2-0. An hour after the Final was completed the Wanderers Reserves took to the field for a Lancashire Combination game, defeating Lostock Hall 4-1.

After the end of the first season the centre position of the ground, which had sunk during the bad weather, was raised in the hope that it would withstand future downpours. During July 1896, Mr A.H.Downs, the club secretary who had seen through the removal from Pikes Lane to Burnden Park, resigned and his place was taken by Mr Frank Bretell, who had been a player and secretary at Everton.

Fog and mist from the River Croal was an eternal problem during the winter for the ground but the first occasion that it had effect on football was on 7 November 1896. Then a First Division encounter with Everton had to be abandoned after an hour's play with neither side having scored.

The first non-English side to play at Burnden were Scottish club Motherwell. They visited on Christmas Day 1896 to take their share of the gate that had been a part of a £40 transfer deal for goalkeeper Paddy Smith. A festive crowd of 4,000 saw Bolton win 6-0.

In January 1897 Burnden hosted the 'World' mile running championship. A crowd of 1,000 were present to see J.Craig win the race in a time of 4 minutes 30.25 seconds to win the £100 prize.

6 February 1897 saw Burnden host what was advertised as the 400 yards championship of the world. A crowd of 9,007 paid £297 to see E.C.Bredin and A.R.Downer run against one another. It was Downer who took the £100 prize with a winning time of 44.45 seconds for the one-lap event.

On 13 March 1897 the ground was introduced to a different sport. Prior to the League game with Burnley a lacrosse match took place that saw Bolton defeat North Manchester 1-0. The following month the first professional sports meeting at the ground took place. Unfortunately the event had to be postponed for a week due to the terrible weather but when it did take place it attracted a 6,000 crowd.

A crowd of 3,000 soaked up the sun on 14 August 1897 to see the National Cyclists Union 50-mile championship on the cement track.

The ground was alive with the sound of music in May 1898. A crowd of 2,000 attended a local brass band contest!

Wolverhampton Wanderers were the first club to defeat the Trotters in an FA Cup-tie at Burnden. This came on 1 February 1899 with the visitors winning 1-0 in a first-round replay. Four days later Bolton were due to entertain Everton in a First Division game. A crowd of over 5,000 were already in the ground when it was announced that the visitors were refusing to play on the hard lumpy ground and so the game was postponed.

The ground's record receipts increased to £740 on 23 March 1899 when 20,000 saw a replayed FA Cup semi-final tie between Liverpool and Sheffield United. The game ended in a 4-4 draw, after extra-time, with Sheffield United eventually winning through in a third replay at Derby. The Blades went on to win the Cup that year, ironically against Derby at the Crystal Palace.

Burnden played host to the Lancashire Cup Final on 25 March 1899 with the home club taking on fellow First Division side Bury. A crowd of 3,964 saw the Shakers win 3-1 in what was Bolton's first appearance in the Final since 1894.

After relegation had been suffered for the first time in 1899 a public meeting was held in an attempt to raise £800 to keep the club afloat during the summer. One of the suggestions put forward was that the football club should be closed down and the stadium be turned over for sole athletic use.

On 28 October 1899 the first overseas side to were welcomed on to Burnden Park. A crowd of 1,500 saw the Wanderers defeat the Kaffirs, a South African touring side, by 13-3. Hugh Morgan scored four of the goals in what was a 'farcical game', even goalkeeper John Sutcliffe managing to find the net.

Burnden was selected to host the English League against the Irish League in November 1899, this despite the fact that the Wanderers at the time were a Second Division club. Wanderers half-back Jack Fitchett was selected for the English League, being the only representative from the Second Division and also the youngest player.

The first Bolton player to score a League hat-trick at Burnden was Laurie Bell who got his share during a 7-0 Second Division defeat of Loughborough Town on 30 December 1899. The following April he became the first Wanderer to hit four goals in a game at Burnden, this time in a 5-0 win over Burton Swifts as Bolton won

promotion as runners-up to Sheffield Wednesday.

The only occasion that Burnden Park has been selected to host an FA Cup Final was on 27 April 1901. Then, Tottenham Hotspur defeated Sheffield United 3-1 in what was a replay, the crowd being only 20,470.

The first Bolton player to be sent off at Burnden was goalkeeper Jack Sutcliffe on 18 January 1902 in a First Division game against Sheffield Wednesday. Sutcliffe had disputed a Wednesday goal, claiming that the scorer, Davis, had pushed both himself and the ball into the back of the net. The custodian was eventually sent off for the use of bad language and full-back Charlie Ostick went into goal as Bolton ran out 3-1 winners.

During April 1902 Burnden hosted games to raise money for the Ibrox disaster. 26 people having lost their lives after terracing had collapsed during a Scotland against England international. The Bolton bakers took on the Bolton chimney sweeps whilst the Wanderers faced old foes Preston North End.

The Bank Holiday weekend of August 1904 saw the club's 18th and final amateur athletic festival. A crowd of 8,000 saw a total of 1,037 entries at differing events with prizes totalling £200. And so the event that had opened the ground in 1895 came to an end.

On 19 November 1904 both Sam Marsh and Walter White recorded hat-tricks in the 7-1 Second Division win over Burton United.

In the summer of 1905 the first major change to the ground took place with the dismantling of the cycling track and the erection of the Manchester Road Stand at a cost of £3,658. This would provide accommodation for 6,000 spectators, 3,420 seated, 2,000 on the terrace and 580 along the track.

During the summer of 1906, 32 terraces were laid on the slope of the Embankment and the Great Lever End was also terraced.

Burnden Park hosted its second FA Cup semi-final on 23 March 1907 when Everton took on West Bromwich Albion. Everton had already won an FA Cup-tie at Burnden that season, having defeated the Wanderers 3-0 in a third-round replay a month earlier. It proved to be a lucky omen as the Toffees ran out 2-1 winners but went down to Sheffield Wednesday in the Final at Crystal Palace.

Sam Marsh scored Bolton's first FA Cup hat-trick at Burnden on 22 February 1908 yet it wasn't enough to win a third-round tie against Everton. The game ended 3-3 with Everton winning the replay 3-1 after extra-time at Goodison.

Burnden Park in 1914 before the addition of the wing stand to the Manchester Road side.

In December 1910 the Wanderers played three Second Division League games on Burnden. All were won with centre-forward Billy Hughes scoring a hat-trick in each game. In the first game of the New Year at Burnden the Wanderers defeated Barnsley but Hughes only managed to score twice!

On 2 September 1911, the opening day of the League season, Newcastle United were the visitors when the Manchester Road Stand caught fire. Fortunately this was quickly extinguished with little damage and the cause was found to be a discarded cigarette.

The first Central League game to take place at Burnden was on 9 September 1911 when the Wanderers drew 0-0 with Burslem Port Vale.

During the summer of 1912 the Great Lever side of the ground was covered to enable spectators to watch football on three sides under shelter from the elements.

On 29 November 1913 Burnden Park attracted its first League attendance of over 50,000. 53,747 paid then record receipts of £1,700 to see the Wanderers defeat First Division leaders Blackburn Rovers by virtue of a goal from George Lillycrop.

In July 1914, the Gas Committee recommended to the Town Council that Burnden Park be sold to the football club at a cost of £8,021. Although the club had no intention of building a second Hampden Park, it was necessary to keep the large space between the ground and the main Manchester Road clear and free from new buildings to facilitate the gathering of large crowds.

During 1915, the Wing Stand was added on to the Manchester Road side of the ground.

Dublin Bohemians were the first Irish club side to visit Burnden. This was for a friendly on 28 April 1920 when they ran out 4-2 winners.

The club's first ever League game to take place in the month of May came at Burnden in 1920. The Trotters defeated Middlesbrough 2-1 to finish in sixth spot in Division One.

World War One saw the ground fall from grace with the wooden steps on the Embankment side rotting. In June 1920 these were replaced with terraced flags which made for a much firmer footing.

The visit of League leaders Burnley, who had gone 27 games without defeat, on 5 March 1921 attracted a paid attendance of 54,809. Although there are no accurate records of the season ticket attendance there would be over 57,000 on the ground which stood as the best League attendance at Burnden until 1938.

In June 1921 the Wing Stand (now known as 'A' block) on the Manchester Road side was erected. Season tickets were made available in that area at a cost of £4 10s (£4.50p) whilst a ladies season ticket cost £3.

On 28 March 1925 the Trotters took on Manchester City in a friendly at Burnden. Nothing unusual in that, except for the fact that both sides were taking part in a new offside proposal. A crowd of 4,621 saw the game played with no offsides awarded within 40 yards from goal. Bolton ran out 3-0 winners with goals from Idwal Davies, David Jack and Joe Smith, all of which came in a ten-minute first-half spell.

On 7 February 1927 Burnden hosted an England trial match. England were defeated 3-2 by The Rest with three Wanderers players involved. Jimmy Seddon represented England, whilst Dick

Six Wanderers sprinting around the rear of Burnden Park in 1933. From left to right are Taylor, Eastham, Milsom, Westwood, Rimmer and Halford. That year a massive crowd of 69,912 – still the ground record and now, of course, never to be exceeded, watched an FA Cup-tie against Manchester City.

Pym and Harry Nuttall played for The Rest before a crowd of 14,002.

During 1927 the club turned down the opportunity to use the ground for greyhound racing and the BBC were refused permission to broadcast a League match.

On 5 November 1927 the Wanderers' seven goals against Burnley were shared between two players, Harold Blackmore and David Jack with the former grabbing four.

The club's offices moved to Burnden Park in September 1928 having previously been situated in the town centre at Oxford Street.

During 1928 the Burnden Stand was built on the Darcy Lever side of the ground at a cost of £17,712. The seating area held 2,750 whilst the paddock wasn't completed until August 1929. The structure has hardly changed in its 66-year existence.

On 18 February 1933 Burnden held its highest official attendance when Manchester City visited for a fifth-round FA Cup-tie. The attendance of 69,912 was made up in the different areas of the ground as follows.

Opposite page, bottom: The frontage of Burnden Park which gave L.S.Lowry the inspiration to paint *The Match* in 1953.

Embankment	28,087
Great Lever End	19,785
A Stand Manchester Road	1,596
B Stand Manchester Road	1,245
D Stand Manchester Road	868
Burnden Stand	2,789
Burnden Paddock	9,469
Manchester Road Paddock	5,494
Track	430
A Stand standing	149

Four days later, on 22 February 1933, the Wanderers entertained Portsmouth in a First Division fixture. A crowd of only 3,101 were in attendance, the lowest ever for a First Division game on the ground and the lowest for a League game until 1985.

In August 1934 the Great Lever corner of the Burnden Stand was partitioned off for exclusive use of youngsters at a cost of 6d each (2Σp) with a capacity of 500 seats. The goal-posts were changed for what was to be a promotion winning season, oval shaped posts replacing the old four-sided ones.

The highest attendance on Burnden for a Second Division fixture was 46,554 on 1 May 1935. Champions Brentford were the visitors with Bolton finishing 2-0 winners to set themselves up for the runners-up spot.

In August 1935 the terracing on the corner section of the Burnden and Great Lever sides was extended. Clocks were placed on top of both the stands which had been supplied by brewer's Magees. These remained in use until 1973 on the Burnden Stand and 1975 on the Manchester Road stand.

The record League attendance at Burnden was set on 15 October 1938, 54,564 watching the Wanderers defeat League leaders Everton 4-2, Jack Roberts getting a hat-trick. With season ticket holders added to the paid attendance there would have been over 58,000 on the ground.

On 16 December 1939 Bolton took part in an unusual game against the 53rd Field Regiment Royal Artillery on Burnden. The Bolton side was, Goodall, Eastwood, Hubbick, Whalley, Atkinson,

Nicholson, W.G.A.Jones, Cunliffe, Hunt, Sidebottom, Connor.

The 53rd RA side lined up as, Gunner Hanson, Gunners Winter and Catterall, Sgt Goslin, Gunner Ithell, Bombardiers Hurst and Geldard, Gunners Sinclair, Howe, Roberts and Thompson.

Incredibly Bolton were practically playing themselves with the Army players having been given leave to take part. A crowd of 1,509 saw the teams draw 3-3. Indeed the 53rd RA went on to play games together all over the world wherever they were stationed.

During World War Two, Burnden Park was commandeered for use by the authorities. The pitch was used by the Education Services whilst the stands were taken over by the Ministry of Supply.

On 3 February 1947 only 4,280 saw Bolton defeat Leeds United 2-0 in a First Division match. This remained as the lowest post-war League attendance on the ground until November 1985.

Concrete trainers' covers were installed in 1951 and these remained in use until 1986 by which time an area in the Manchester Road Paddock had been handed over for managers and substitutes along with a disabled spectators area.

In 1953 L.S.Lowry used the car-park and the Main Stand as the backdrop for his painting entitled The Match.

Burnden was used in the 1954 film, Love Match, staring Arthur Askey in which a train

The Wanderers representing the 53rd RA. Back row (left to right):
D.Winter,
H.Goslin,
S.Hanson,
G.Cotterall,
J.Ithell, J.Hurst.
Front row:
A.Geldard,
D.Howe,
R.Westwood,
J.H.Roberts,
T.Sinclair.

An unusual Bolton line-up. In April 1960 the Wanderers faced England on Burnden in a game lasting 20 minutes each way. England wore Bolton's home kit and won 2-0 with goals from Peter Broadbent and Joe Baker. Back row (left to right): Jimmy Armfield (later to manage Wanderers), Bill Slater, Ron Flowers, Ron Springett, Ray Parry (Wanderers), Ray Wilson. Front row: John Connelly, Peter Broadbent, Ronnie Clayton, Joe Baker, Bobby Charlton.

driver pulls up on the Embankment End to watch the game in progress.

The last League match to take place on the ground on Christmas Day was in 1954 when Tottenham won 2-1, Dennis Stevens scoring for the Trotters.

The only FA Charity Shield game to have taken place on the ground came on 6 October 1958 when Bolton, who were the FA Cup holders, defeated the League champions, Wolverhampton Wanderers, 4-1. The crowd was 15,239.

The first European side to play on Burnden Park were CDSA Moscow who visited on 4 November 1957 for a game under the floodlights.

Bolton's post-war crowd record came on 14 February 1959 when Preston North End were the visitors for a fifth-round FA Cup-tie; 58,692 saw a 2-2 draw with the Wanderers finally getting through in a second replay at Ewood Park.

The only French side to have played on Burnden are Le Havre. They visited on 15 March 1961 for the second leg of the Friendship Cup. The sides had drawn 1-1 in France and Bolton took the Cup by winning 4-0.

During 1961 the gymnasium at the rear of the Burnden Stand was built which enabled the players to use those inside facilities rather than underneath the stand itself.

The first German side to play on Burnden Park were Saarbrucken. This was on 22 November 1961, the Trotters winning the friendly 4-1 to gain revenge for a 1-0 defeat in Germany the previous May.

Nat Lofthouse scored the Wanderers' first hat-trick in the Football League Cup on 26 October 1960. This came in a second-round tie during a 6-2 defeat of Grimsby Town. These were to be the only goals scored in the competition by 'The Lion of Vienna'.

RFC Liege came to Burnden for a friendly on 3 December 1962 to become the first Belgian side to play on the ground. A crowd of 6,498 saw Bolton win 3-2 with Ron McGarry scoring one of the goals in what was his last appearance for the club.

Burnden Park hosted its third FA Cup semi-final on 23 April 1966 when Everton defeated Manchester United by 1-0. As in 1907, when Everton won a semi at Burnden, they went on to face Sheffield Wednesday in the Final. On this occasion they went on to win the Cup by 3-2 after being two down.

In 1967 the frontage of the ground was extended to accommodate a supporters' club. This was originally built as first-floor premises with a drive through underneath but was later boxed in to create offices.

The only recorded instance of Burnden Park

being used for a cricket match was in May 1969 when a Lancashire XI took on a Wanderers XI in aid of Eddie Hopkinson's testimonial. Drivers on Manchester Road had to take care as Clive Lloyd smashed a number of sixes way out of the ground.

Burnden Park kicked off its earliest League

season in 1969 when, on 9 August, they defeated Millwall 4-1, John Byrom netting a hat-trick.

Manchester United were involved in Burnden's last FA Cup semi-final in 1970. They took on Leeds United in a second replay after goalless games at both Hillsborough and Villa Park. A crowd of 56,000 saw Leeds win the tie thanks to a second-half Billy Bremner goal, although they lost the Final in a replay to Chelsea. The crowd paid then record receipts of £42,000 which stood until the Wanderers faced Everton in the 1977 League Cup semi-final second leg.

In February 1971 a Burnden landmark was destroyed by fire. The railway signal box on the Embankment behind the scoreboard caught fire and was badly damaged. The box was later demolished.

On 1 March 1971 a crowd of 943 saw the Wanderers defeat Rangers Freja, the first Danish side to come to Burnden, by 2-1. The Danish side fielded a 'keeper by the name of Bone who wore spectacles, his task made all the harder as the game was played in a snowstorm. This proved to be Paul Fletcher's final game for Bolton before his transfer to Burnley.

The semi-final of the FA Amateur Cup was held at Burnden on 20 March 1971 between Skelmersdale United and Leatherhead. A crowd of 7,985 saw United win through 2-0 to face Dagenham in the Wembley Final which they won by 4-1.

Czech side Bohemians of Prague were pre-season visitors to Burnden in August 1972. The Wanderers came from behind to draw 1-1.

During a game against Rochdale on 17 March 1973, which the Wanderers won 2-1, both linesmen were situated on the Burnden side. Referee, Ron Tinkler, ordered both linesmen to patrol the one line for the last half-hour of the match. Mr Butcher, of Kendal, made his pioneering journey across the park to share the line with colleague Mr Brown, of Liverpool. The referee explained that he was unable to see his linesmen on the Manchester Road side due to the sun.

The highest Burnden crowd for a Third Division fixture came against Blackburn Rovers on 28 March 1973. Rovers won 1-0 to inflict the Wanderers' only home League defeat that term, before 33,010.

Burnden witnessed its first ever game on a Sunday on 6 January 1974 when the Trotters defeated Stoke City 3-2 in the third round of the FA Cup. A fortnight later Bristol City went down

9 August 1969 and John Byrom sets Bolton on their way to a 4-1 opening day win over Millwall. It was the earliest date in a season on which Burnden has staged a Football League game.

The Embankment crowd for the last FA Cup semi-final to be played on the ground, in 1970 between Manchester United and Leeds United.

177

2-1 in the first Sunday League game on the ground.

Fences were first installed on the ground in June 1977, initially behind each goal, they were eight feet high and cost £17,000. This came after pitch invasions, notably in promotion clashes against Chelsea in February 1977 and Wolves in May 1977. The ground was completely fenced in the summer of 1979.

Crowd segregation came into force for the first time on 29 April 1978 against Fulham, a 0-0 draw earning Bolton a point that secured the Second Division championship.

In the summer of 1978 the Great Lever End was seated with a facility for 4,342 spectators.

Perhaps the most attractive pre-season game at Burnden came on 13 August 1979 when Ajax Amsterdam were the visitors. The Dutch side ran out 3-1 winners in the pouring rain with the Wanderers' goal coming from a penalty by Alan Gowling. Gowling also missed a penalty that had to be retaken, Neil Whatmore then hitting the post, whilst Lerby also missed from the spot for Ajax.

In the close season of 1980 undersoil heating was installed at Burnden. The system was of a Swedish design and operated by way of an oil-driven boiler feeding an undersoil network of hot water pipes. The cost was around £70,000 for the 14 miles of heating pipes which were placed under the pitch at the same time as major remedial work on levelling and draining took place.

Polish side Legia Warsaw came to Burnden for a pre-season game in August 1980. Wanderers' Polish winger Tadeusz Nowak couldn't prevent his former club from winning 2-0.

The lowest attendance for a Second Division game on Burnden was 4,631 for the visit of Cambridge United on 23 April 1983. The Wanderers won 2-0 but the goals were to be their last at that level until 1993.

Tony Caldwell became the only player to score five goals in a League game at Burnden on 10 September 1983. This came during Bolton's 8-1 defeat of Walsall in the Third Division.

Another Burnden landmark was demolished in 1984, the half-time scoreboard on the Embankment falling into disrepair, having been in use since the late 1940s.

In October 1985 the go-ahead was given for a multi-million pound development on the Embankment side of the ground which was to include a superstore. The scheme would see the Wanderers receive a substantial amount but the deal included converting the pitch from grass to artificial. The club were given permission to switch to plastic but in January 1987 the League voted on a freeze on the spread of artificial pitches and so Burnden remained covered in 'real grass'.

Burnden Park's lowest ever League attendance came on 5 November 1985. Only 2,902 saw a Third Division game against Darlington which ended in a 3-0 win for the visitors.

Towards the end of 1986 the then 16,000 capacity Embankment was cut in half as work began to accommodate the Normid Superstore on the site of the 1946 disaster.

Perhaps the biggest upset on Burnden came in November 1986 but didn't involve the Wanderers, not Bolton Wanderers at any rate. Multipart League side Chorley were drawn at home in the first round of the FA Cup to face Fourth Division Wolverhampton Wanderers. Their ground at Victory Park was unable to hold the anticipated attendance and so the game was switched to Burnden. A 1-1 draw resulted and with an identical score at Molineux the second replay came back to Burnden. A crowd of 5,421 saw the Magpies embarrass Wolves by winning 3-0.

Peterborough United were the visitors for Burnden's lowest attendance (3,746) for a Fourth Division game on 31 August 1987. Bolton won the game 2-0.

Burnden's highest crowd for a Fourth Division game was 9,921 on 4 April 1988 when the Wanderers defeated Burnley 2-1.

John Thomas scored Bolton's only Burnden hat-trick in the Fourth Division on 23 April 1988 during the club's 6-0 win over Newport County.

The lowest Burnden attendance for a first-class game came on 10 December 1991. Then, only 1,507 saw the Wanderers defeat Rochdale 4-1 in a preliminary Autoglass Trophy tie. The stay-aways missed a hat-trick from David Reeves, the only one scored by the striker whilst at Bolton.

On 24 January 1993 the first big screen telecast of a Wanderers away game was transmitted to

Burnden Park's lowest attendance for a first-class game saw 1,507 witness David Reeves' hat-trick. This is one of his goals during the 4-1 defeat of Rochdale in the Autoglass Trophy. The goalkeeper on the ground is former Wanderer Kevin Rose.

Burnden. A 5,000 crowd saw pictures from the fourth round FA Cup-tie against Wolves at Molineux which Bolton won 2-0. The exercise was repeated for the next round when Derby County ended Cup hopes as Wanderers crashed to a 3-1 defeat at the Baseball Ground.

In the close season of 1993, Burnden Park moved into a new era with the installation of an electronic scoreboard, capable of giving out messages and advertisements.

On 5 March 1994 John McGinlay scored a hat-trick for Bolton in their 3-2 First Division defeat of

January 1993 and Burnden's spectators see an away game on a large TV screen.

Burnden Park at the start of the 1994-95 season – the ground's 100th – looking towards the Embankment.

The forecourt of Burnden Park.

Charlton Athletic to become the first player to complete the feat both for and against the Wanderers at Burnden. In March 1991 he had scored all of Bury's goals in their 3-1 win over Bolton.

In the summer of 1994 the 8ft fences around the ground were reduced to stomach-high with the exception of the visitors' section.

On 8 March 1995 John McGinlay struck Bolton's 100th League Cup goal at Burnden to send the club to Wembley for the first time in the competition. His effort came two minutes from time to give the Trotters a 4-3 aggregate win against Swindon Town.

Looking towards the Manchester Road Stand.

Playing Record at Burnden Park
Football League Record, Pikes Lane/Burnden Park split

	Played	Won	Drawn	Lost	For	Against	Points
Pikes Lane Division One	91	57	10	24	243	140	239
Burnden Park Division One (Premier from 1992/93)	1063	569	243	251	2013	1249	1266
Division Two(inc 1 Play-off) (Div One from 1992/93)	493	288	100	105	941	463	720
Division Three (inc 3 Play-offs) (Div Two from 1992/93)	256	139	63	54	392	213	446
Division Four (Div Three from 1992/93)	23	15	6	2	42	12	51
Total	1926	1068	422	436	3631	2077	2722
Burnden Total	1835	1011	412	412	3388	1937	2483

Aerial view of
Burnden Park
in the 1960s

Bolton Wanderers Football Club
Football League Record at Burnden Park

	Played	Won	Drawn	Lost	For	Against	Position	Division
1895-96	15	12	2	1	34	14	4	1
1896-97	15	7	3	5	22	18	8	1
1897-98	15	9	2	4	18	13	11	1
1898-99	17	6	5	6	24	21	17	1
1899-00	17	14	2	1	47	7	2	2
1900-01	17	10	5	2	21	12	10	1
1901-02	17	10	6	1	38	17	12	1
1902-03	17	6	2	9	18	20	18	1
1903-04	17	10	3	4	38	11	7	2
1904-05	17	15	0	2	53	16	2	2
1905-06	19	13	1	5	51	22	6	1
1906-07	19	10	4	5	35	18	6	1
1907-08	19	10	3	6	35	26	19	1
1908-09	19	14	3	2	37	8	1	2
1909-10	19	7	2	10	31	34	20	1
1910-11	19	17	2	0	53	12	2	2
1911-12	19	14	2	3	35	15	4	1
1912-13	19	10	6	3	36	20	8	1
1913-14	19	13	4	2	41	14	6	1
1914-15	19	8	5	6	35	27	17	1
1919-20	21	11	3	7	35	29	6	1
1920-21	21	15	6	0	53	17	3	1
1921-22	21	12	4	5	40	24	6	1
1922-23	21	11	8	2	36	17	13	1
1923-24	21	13	6	2	45	13	4	1
1924-25	21	18	2	1	61	13	3	1
1925-26	21	11	6	4	46	31	8	1

	Played	Won	Drawn	Lost	For	Against	Position	Division
1926-27	21	15	5	1	54	19	4	1
1927-28	21	12	5	4	47	26	7	1
1928-29	21	10	6	5	44	25	14	1
1929-30	21	11	5	5	46	24	15	1
1930-31	21	12	6	3	45	26	14	1
1931-32	21	15	1	5	51	25	17	1
1932-33	21	10	7	4	49	33	21	1
1933-34	21	14	2	5	45	22	3	2
1934-35	21	17	1	3	63	15	2	2
1935-36	21	11	4	6	41	27	13	1
1936-37	21	6	6	9	22	33	20	1
1937-38	21	11	6	4	38	22	7	1
1938-39	21	10	6	5	39	35	8	1
1946-47	21	8	5	8	30	28	18	1
1947-48	21	11	2	8	29	25	17	1
1948-49	21	10	4	7	43	32	14	1
1949-50	21	10	5	6	34	22	16	1
1950-51	21	11	2	8	31	20	8	1
1951-52	21	11	7	3	35	26	5	1
1952-53	21	9	4	8	39	35	14	1
1953-54	21	14	6	1	45	20	5	1
1954-55	21	11	6	4	45	20	18	1
1955-56	21	13	3	5	50	24	8	1
1956-57	21	13	6	2	42	23	9	1
1957-58	21	9	5	7	38	35	15	1
1958-59	21	14	3	4	56	30	4	1
1959-60	21	12	5	4	37	27	6	1
1960-61	21	9	5	7	38	29	18	1
1961-62	21	11	7	3	35	22	11	1
1962-63	21	13	3	5	35	18	18	1
1963-64	21	6	5	10	30	35	21	1
1964-65	21	13	6	2	46	17	3	2
1965-66	21	12	2	7	43	25	9	2
1966-67	21	10	7	4	36	19	9	2
1967-68	21	8	6	7	37	28	12	2
1968-69	21	8	7	6	29	26	17	2
1969-70	21	9	6	6	31	23	16	2
1970-71	21	6	5	10	22	31	22	2
1971-72	23	11	8	4	25	13	7	3
1972-73	23	18	4	1	44	9	1	3
1973-74	21	12	5	4	30	17	11	2
1974-75	21	9	7	5	27	16	10	2
1975-76	21	12	5	4	36	14	4	2
1976-77	21	15	2	4	46	21	4	2
1977-78	21	16	4	1	39	14	1	2
1978-79	21	10	5	6	36	28	17	1
1979-80	21	5	11	5	19	21	22	1
1980-81	21	10	5	6	40	27	18	2
1981-82	21	10	4	7	28	24	19	2
1982-83	21	10	2	9	30	26	22	2
1983-84	23	13	4	6	36	17	10	3
1984-85	23	12	5	6	38	22	17	3
1985-86	23	10	4	9	35	30	18	3
1986-87	24	8	6	10	31	28	21	3*
1987-88	23	15	6	2	42	12	3	4
1988-89	23	12	8	3	42	23	10	3
1989-90	24	12	8	4	33	20	6	3*
1990-91	24	15	5	4	34	18	4	3*
1991-92	23	10	9	4	26	19	13	3
1992-93	23	18	2	3	48	14	2	2‡
1993-94	23	10	8	5	40	31	14	1
1994-95	24	17	6	1	45	13	3	14*
	1835	1011	412	412	3388	1937		

* Including one Play-off game
‡ Division changes

Bolton Wanderers FA Cup Record at Burnden Park

Bolton's first 20 games in the FA Cup competition on home soil took place at Pikes Lane. During that period they scored no less than 89 goals in those games including the record 13-0 victory over Sheffield United in the second round of 1890.

Only Notts County and Preston managed to win FA Cup-ties at Pikes Lane and, indeed, the Wanderers could boast to being unbeaten in home FA Cup-ties between 1887 and 1898.

Bolton's best FA Cup wins at Burnden have been by 6-1, against Brighton in 1934, and 5-0 against Woking in 1908 and Liverpool in 1946.

On the other hand, the heaviest defeat has been by 5-0 by Bristol City in 1903 and Manchester City in 1937. Perhaps one of their most successful periods in the competition at Burnden has been in recent history. After going out of the Cup to Port Vale in the 1988-89 season, the Wanderers didn't lose there again until March 1994 when Oldham won a sixth-round tie. That was an unbeaten spell of 12 games that included visits from some of the most illustrious teams in the country.

The Wanderers FA Cup record at Burnden is: Played 136, won 74, drawn 31, lost 31, goals for 245, goals against 151.

Bolton Wanderers League Cup Record at Burnden Park

The Wanderers can point to only two really successful seasons in the competition that began back in 1960. These were in season 1976-77 when the semi-finals were reached and in 1994-95 when the club got to Wembley.

Despite these facts there have been a number of giantkilling acts that brought pleasure to the Burnden Park crowd. The defeats of Liverpool in 1967 and Manchester City in 1971 rank as high as any in the club's history and are much more likely to linger in the memory due to the shocks that the results caused.

The Wanderers have never won a League Cup-tie by more than a four-goal margin and they managed this feat in the first two ties at Burnden in 1960. Hull were defeated 5-1 and Grimsby 6-2. In 1977 Swansea City went down 5-1, in 1982 Carlisle lost 4-0 and the most recent case was in 1989 when Rochdale crumbled 5-1 after winning the first leg at Spotland 2-1.

The heaviest defeat suffered by Bolton at Burnden came in November 1971 when eventual Finalists, Chelsea, won 6-0 in the fourth round after the sides had drawn 1-1 at Stamford Bridge.

The Wanderers League Cup record at Burnden is:
Played 55, won 27, drawn 12, lost 16, goals for 100, goals against 80.

Bolton Wanderers in the Anglo Competitions at Burnden Park

Between 1976 and 1979, Bolton Wanderers took part in the Anglo Scottish Cup, which was a pre-season tournament run on a league basis, followed by a knock-out tournament during the season.

The Wanderers' first game in the competition was on 7 August 1976 when 9,402 spectators were at Burnden to see a goalless draw against Blackpool. Three days later Burnden was once again the venue as Bolton defeated Blackburn Rovers 2-0 with goals from John Byrom and Willie Morgan.

Despite losing their third game, at Burnley, the Wanderers qualified for the quarter-finals where they played Partick Thistle over two legs. At Burnden a scoreless draw resulted but the Scottish side went through by winning the game at Firhill.

Bolton failed to qualify during 1977 and 1978, although there was a rare sight at Burnden in August 1978 when Oldham Athletic were the visitors. The game ended scoreless but Frank Worthington, who was to be that term's leading First Division goalgetter, missed a penalty.

The knock-out stages were again reached in 1979 when the Wanderers faced St Mirren. Having gone down 4-2 at Love Street, Bolton pulled back the arrears at Burnden, forcing extra-time thanks to two goals by Sam Allardyce. The Scottish side managed to hit a winner during that period, ending Bolton's interest in their final game in the competition.

The Wanderers entered the Anglo-Italian Cup in 1993, qualifying for the Italian stages by defeating Tranmere at Prenton Park and Sunderland at Burnden. Ancona were the first Italian side to visit Burnden on 12 October 1993, Bolton running out 5-0

winners before 3,448 spectators. The following month a crowd of 3,021 were at Burnden for the visit of Brescia. The Italian side included Romanian international Gheorghe Hagi in their line-up and he went on to produce a memorable performance in a game that ended 3-3.

Bolton then remained unbeaten on visits to both Pisa and Ascoli but failed to qualify for the Wembley Final.

Bolton's Burnden record in the Anglo-Scottish Cup:
Played 9, won 5, drawn 4, lost 0, goals for 10, goals against 3.
Bolton's Burnden record in the Anglo-Italian Cup:
Played 2, won 1, drawn 1, lost 0, goals for 8, goals against 3.

Alan Thompson heads Wanderers' third goal in the 5-0 Anglo-Italian Cup win over Ancona at Burnden in October 1993.

Bolton Wanderers in the Lancashire Senior Cup at Burnden Park

Bolton Wanderers took part in the Lancashire Senior Cup from its inception in 1879-80. Their first opponents were Bolton All Saints, who were defeated 5-2 at Pikes Lane.

The club were victorious in two Finals before moving to Burnden Park. In 1886 they took the trophy by virtue of a 1-0 win over Blackburn Rovers at Deepdale and then in 1891 defeated Darwen 3-1 at Everton. During this period the Trotters recorded some of their largest ever victories at any level. Wigan were thrashed 14-0, Low Moor 13-0 and Blackburn Olympic 11-2.

Burnley were the first visitors to Burnden for a

Lancashire Cup-tie on 19 January 1896, the Clarets winning the first-round tie 2-1.

It was in 1899 that Bolton first reached the Final of the competition whilst at Burnden. The game took place on home soil with only 3,964 spectators witnessing Bury's 3-1 win in what was a relegation season. Tom McAteer scored the Trotters' goal.

In 1903-04, the season that Wanderers got to the FA Cup Final, non-League St Helens put them out of the Lancashire Cup at Burnden in a first-round replay.

The trophy wasn't on show in the Wanderers

boardroom again until 1912 when revenge was gained against Burnley in a Final tie played at Turf Moor.

It probably comes as no surprise that the club's most successful period in the competition came during the 1920s when Bolton were known as the 'Cup kings of England'.

In 1921 they reached the Final, only to go down 2-0 to Manchester City at Old Trafford. In 1922 Bolton brought the Cup back with a 3-1 defeat of Bury at Gigg Lane. Finally, in 1925, Burnden witnessed a Bolton win in the Final and in 1927 a John Smith goal against Bury before 13,229 Burndenites allowed Jimmy Seddon to lift the trophy aloft.

The Wanderers' best victory at Burnden came in November 1931 when Liverpool were taken to task by eight goals to one with Billy Butler netting four times. The unusual thing about this was that in the final League game of the season, Liverpool visited Burnden and lost by exactly the same score, Jack Milsom getting four on that occasion. That season ended with Bolton again becoming Lancashire Cup holders when Manchester City were beaten 3-2 at Maine Road.

1933 saw the Wanderers again reach the Final, only to go down 2-1 to Liverpool at Anfield, but a year later the trophy returned to Burnden with a 4-2 win over Oldham at Maine Road.

After the war, many clubs saw the competition only as a secondary event, fielding reserve sides with Bolton winning it for the last time for 40 years in 1948. A year earlier the Wanderers had taken part in a first-round tie with Manchester City that had gone to four games. Only one was played at Burnden but Bolton got through only to lose in the semi-final against Bury. In 1964-65 this feat of four games to settle a tie was equalled when Blackpool eventually won a first-round tie.

Non-League Chorley ended Bolton's interests in the first round in both 1972 and 1973, the latter being at Burnden, although the semi-finals were reached in the competition's final season in 1973, Manchester City winning 3-2 at Burnden.

The competition was reintroduced in 1982 under the sponsorship of the Isle of Man Tourist Board as a pre-season tournament. Bolton's first game was a 3-2 reverse at Preston swiftly followed by a 1-0 home defeat by Blackburn.

Bolton failed to qualify from the first six of the new style competitions but this changed in 1988. Having won the first two games they then reached the Final by defeating Rochdale 5-4 on penalties at Burnden thanks to a save from goalkeeper Gareth Gray who failed to make a League appearance for the Trotters. A John Thomas goal won the trophy for Bolton before their own supporters against Preston to bridge that 40-year gap. 1990 produced a repeat of the Final from 1988 with Burnden again witnessing a Bolton success, David Reeves scoring both goals in a 2-1 win.

The last Lancashire Cup-tie played at the ground was in July 1993 when 3,091 saw John McGinlay score Bolton's goal in a 3-1 defeat by Blackpool. Since then the Wanderers have preferred to opt out of the competition due to their tight schedule.

Bolton's overall record in the competition at Burden is:

Played 119, won 68, drawn 15, lost 36, goals for 259, goals against 165.

The Wanderers side that won the Lancashire Cup in 1988 – the first time for 40 years. From left to right: Cowdrill, Savage, Gray, Storer, Stevens, Darby, Winstanley, Henshaw, Thompson, Crombie, Felgate, Brookman, Came, Brown, Thomas.

Bolton Wanderers in the Manchester Senior Cup at Burnden Park

The Manchester Senior Cup was instituted in 1885 but the Wanderers did not enter until their first season of Manchester FA membership in 1891-92. The trophy was first won in the last season at Pikes Lane when Bury were defeated 3-2 in the Final at Hyde Road.

In January 1897 the first Manchester Senior Cup-tie on Burnden saw Bolton defeat Fairfield by 3-0. Once again the Final was reached and this time Bury took the trophy by winning 3-1, again at Hyde Road.

At the turn of the century the Wanderers had relegated the competition to the Reserves with a sprinkling of first-team players.

Finals held on the ground involving Bolton Wanderers took place in 1921 (Manchester United being defeated 2-0) and 1948 (Manchester United winning 3-1 after extra-time).

The last tie played at the ground came during season 1956-57 when Oldham Athletic won a semi-final game. The competition later became a one-off Final between two of the members, Bolton's last game being in 1963 when the trophy was won with a 3-1 defeat of Oldham Athletic at Boundary Park. The competition was last played for in 1965.

Bolton's best-ever score in the competition came at Burnden in January 1926 when Eccles United were beaten 9-0, whilst the heaviest defeat came at the hands of Manchester City, who won 9-3 at the same venue in February 1899.

Bolton's overall record in the competition at Burnden Park is:
Played 48, won 29, drawn 5, lost 14, goals for 125, goals against 61.

Bolton Wanderers in the Lancashire FA Youth Cup at Burnden Park

Bolton Wanderers were the first winners of the Lancashire FA Youth Cup when, in March 1971, they defeated Blackpool at Burnden in the Final.

Having got the better of both Oldham Athletic and Manchester United at Burnden to reach the Final, things appeared to be going against them when the Seasiders were winning 3-1 with five minutes remaining. But Paul Jones pulled one back and two minutes from time Peter Lucas equalised to send the 5,000 crowd wild with delight. Three minutes into the first period of extra-time Stuart Lee converted a penalty to make sure the trophy came to Burnden Park.

The following season Bolton again reached the Final but on this occasion it was played over two legs against Manchester United. At Old Trafford, United won 2-1 and followed this up with a 3-2 win at Burnden before 3,266 to take the cup, Sam Allardyce and Neil Whatmore scoring for the Wanderers.

In 1975, Bolton reached the semi-finals before losing 5-4 on penalties to Everton at Burnden after two goalless games.

Bolton won the trophy again in 1978, defeating Manchester United 2-0 at Old Trafford and 4-0 at Burnden, this coming the day after the club had been presented with the Second Division championship trophy.

One of the most bizarre games in the competition took place at Burnden against Manchester City in February 1981 at the semi-final stage. City lost defender Andy May after 28 minutes when he was sent off for a foul on Wayne Foster. The Wanderers then lost

Bolton Wanderers were the first winners of the Lancashire FA Youth Cup in March 1971. They defeated Blackpool 4-3 after extra-time. Captain Don McAllister holds the trophy with Paul Jones and coach George Taylor looking on.

goalkeeper Gary Walker through injury and Foster moved from centre-forward to emergency 'keeper. The game ended scoreless after extra-time and both sides left the field only to be called back to settle the issue on penalties. City went on to win 5-3, the game finishing two hours and 38 minutes after it had started.

Burnden Park again hosted the Final in 1984, Manchester City winning 3-0, but Bolton gained revenge over City in 1987 when they won a semi-final 5-4 on penalties on their way to winning the trophy against Blackburn at Ewood.

Bolton's last success in the competition was in March 1988. Then, they defeated Wigan Athletic 2-0 with goals from Mike Jeffrey and Mark Raven. The Wanderers could even afford the luxury of a missed penalty from Derek Booth.

Bolton's record in the competition at Burnden is:
Played 35, won 19, drawn 4, lost 12, goals for 57, goals against 47.

Bolton Wanderers in the FA Youth Cup at Burnden Park

The FA Youth Cup competition began in season 1952-53 with the Wanderers going out in their first appearance, Bury winning 3-1 in a game that took place at Bromwich Street.

The club's best-ever season came in 1955-56. Everton were the first Burnden visitors in the competition, for what was a fourth-round tie on 1 February 1956. The game took place on a Wednesday afternoon, as the ground was without floodlighting, Bolton winning 4-0 on a frost-bound pitch.

Wolves, who had reached the Final in both 1953 and 1954, were the next visitors to Burnden. Bolton ran out 2-0 winners to reach the two legged semi-finals for the only time.

Neil Whatmore goes close in the FA Youth Cup quarter-final tie against Arsenal in February 1972. Whatmore later went on to score 121 goals in 338 first-class appearances for Bolton.

The Wanderers' opponents were Manchester United, who had won the trophy in it's first three years. The sides drew 1-1 in the first leg at Old Trafford, the return at Burnden taking place on Monday 23 April with a 6.30pm kick-off. A crowd of 24,553 were on Burnden for the tie, Bolton lining up as follows: Dean; Wilson, Edisbury, Stanley, Oxtoby, Edwards, Birch, Deakin, Hart, Bannister, Riley. Manchester United's side was: Hawksworth; Queenan, Jones, Cardon, Holland, McGuiness, Morgans, Pearson, Dawson, Charlton, Fidler.

United managed to keep up their magnificent record in the competition by winning 3-0, Bobby Charlton hitting two of the goals. They went on to win the trophy by defeating Chesterfield 4-3 in the two legged Final.

Although the 1956 youth side went farthest in the competition, the sides from 1972 and 1973 put up good shows with a number making the professional ranks.

In February 1972, Bolton reached the fifth round where they entertained Arsenal. A crowd of 6,230, higher than the previous week's first-team attendance for a Third Division game with Bristol Rovers, saw the Londoners win 1-0. Brian Hornsby hit the winner in the 50th minute. The teams were: Bolton Wanderers: Siddall; Parkinson, Holding, Olinyk, Allardyce, Martin, Taylor, Graham, Whatmore, Smith, Cross. sub: Reid. Arsenal: Horn, Donaldson, Powling, Price, Rixon, Newton, Brady, Williams, Hornsby, Kennerley, Shovelar. Sub: Matthews. Seven of the Bolton side went on to appear for the club in the first team.

The following season the Wanderers got as far as a fourth-round replay where they lost at Ipswich Town. This came after Burnden victories over Wolves, by 6-1, and a New Year's Day defeat of Burnley by 3-0.

Bolton's highest victory in the FA Youth Cup at Burnden came in December 1971 when Halifax Town were thumped 6-0 in the third round.

The club's overall record in the competition at Burnden is:
Played 47, won 26, drawn 6, lost 15, goals for 101, goals against 56.

Bolton in the Central League

Bolton Wanderers were founder members of the Central League in 1911, playing their first game against Liverpool at Anfield. Burslem Port Vale were the first Central League visitors to Burnden, a scoreless draw resulting.

It wasn't until 1954-55 that the Wanderers first secured the championship and forty years later, in Burnden Park's centenary season, the reserves won it for the second time.

The most recent success came by way of steady progress season by season since winning promotion from Division Two in 1991.

Burnden's highest crowd for a reserve fixture came in 1926 when 11,926 attended for the visit of Huddersfield Town.

The Wanderers record win in the competition came at Burnden in April 1994 when Sunderland were defeated 10-1. Both David Lee and Owen Coyle hit hat-tricks before a crowd of 516.

Burnden Park's League of Nations

No less than eight of Wanderers' players that lined up at Burnden for the Play-off semi-final second leg against Wolves in May 1995 had won some sort of international honour.

Never before in the club's history had so many players represented so many different countries.

Goalkeeper Keith Branagan has won Republic of Ireland B honours, whilst both Jason McAteer and Owen Coyle have won full caps for Ireland. All three were on the field at the same time for Ireland's B international with England at Anfield in December 1994. Defender Gudni Bergsson is the captain of Iceland whilst Mixu Paatelainen is a regular for Finland. John McGinlay represents Scotland, Alan Stubbs has an England B cap and Alan Thompson has been selected for the England Under-21 squad.

Added to these are Dutchmen Fabian DeFreitas and Richard Sneekes. Other internationals to represent the Wanderers during 1994-95 were Alan Kernaghan (Northern Ireland) and Peter Shilton (England).

Far left: Finnish international Mixu Paatelainen. *Left:* Republic of Ireland international Jason McAteer salutes the Burnden crowd at the end of the 1993-94 season.

The Future...

During 1994 the club announced plans for a possible move to a purpose-built 25,000 all seater stadium at Horwich.

In many respects Burnden Park has gone full circle in its 100-year history with many of the reasons for leaving Pikes Lane in 1895 applicable in a modern context today. Added to this is the requirement to become all seater.

Wherever the club play in the future all that can be asked is that the first hundred years are as intriguing as Bolton Wanderers' one hundred years at Burnden Park, 1895-1995.

NEW MOVE ON GROUND PLAN

BOLTON Wanderers today took another step towards the crunch decision on whether to stay or leave Burnden Park.

Club officials and the developer of the proposed £40 million sports village at Red Moss met Bolton councillors to report on their progress with a view to lodging an application for outline planning permission early next month.

But Wanderers insist that a decision on the future of Burnden Park has not yet been taken.

Independent consultants have carried out studies covering the impact of the Horwich development on the environment, retail operations and transport. At the same time studies

But Bolton stress no decision yet

By GORDON SHARROCK

have been made and plans drawn up for an all-seater stadium at Burnden Park.

"Our links with the council on both projects have been very encouraging." club chief executive Des McBain explained.

Alternative

"But we will only know that we have an alternative to Burnden Park if and when we have a favourable response to the planning application.

"It would be remiss of us if, in the meantime, we didn't draw up plans for

the future of Burnden Park. If the planning application failed we would have no option but to stay here anyway."

The Sports Village Working Party was told that Wanderers and Orbit, the developers, are now confident that they can satisfy the necessary planning requirements. They have amended plans for the retail section of the ambitious project, which would include a hotel, restaurants, sports hall and leisure facilities as well as a new 25,000 all-seater stadium.

"The developers have gone a long way towards meeting the council's concern over retail," Mr McBain added.

"Subject to a favourable response from the local authority we will be holding further meetings with shareholders and supporters but it must be stressed at this stage that no final decision has yet been taken."

Subscribers

Geoffrey Abey
Michael Ackers
Andrew J Alldred
John Anders
A D Ashton
Mr David Aubrey
Mr Richard Aubrey
G Ball
Michael Bamber
John Barlass
Paul Barlow
Steven Battersby
Ken & Jacqui Beevers
Ian Berry
Kevan Bird
David Blackburn
Darren Lee Boardman
Mrs L J Bown
Mr David Brandwood
Mike Brodrick
David Burton
Jim Butterworth
Alex Carless (Australia)
Donald Carless
John Carney
Jon Carney
Helen, Alan & Thomas Carr
Harry Chadwick
William Chadwick
William N Chadwick
John R J Charlson
Alan Clark
Michael Clarkson
Christopher Collier
Paul Corscadden
Alyn P Coward
Anthony Cranshaw
David Croughton
Andy Cunliffe
Carol Cunniffe
Janet Cutts
John Davidson
Eric William Davies
Christopher M Dawson
Andrew Peter Daynes
Gregory Leonard Dean
Stephen Denham
Harold Dodd
Mr John Dutton
Lee David Eckersley
Grant Anthony Townley Eden
Nathanial R J Eden
Graham Edge

Albert Entwistle
Len Entwistle
Christopher Fairbanks
Mark Edward Fernside
Joseph W Fish
Carl Flitcroft
Sam Fogg
Norman Fort
Kenneth Fullelove
Thomas Fullelove
Alan Gardiner
Rev Keith V Garner
P A Gartside
Desmond Gilroy
Roy Glover
Gregory Goldston
Paul Anthony Gorton
Iain Grace
Ian Gray
Rebecca Green
David Greenhalgh (Helmet)
Tim Greenhalgh
The Gregory Family
Phillip Griffiths
Alan Grundy
Laura Grundy
Mr D F Gudojc
Alan Hale
Gary Hale
Barry Hall
Roy Robert Halliday
Steven Michael Halligan
Shirley A Hallmark
Neil Gary Halton
Vince Hankinson
Steven Hare
Mrs Linda A Hardman
G Hargreaves
Roy Harrison
Gerald Hayes
Joh L Headley
Carol Ann Hemmingway
Mr Peter N Hewitt
Mr Simon W F Hewitt
Andy Heyes
Mark Heys
David K Hill
Ray Hill
Michael F Hodgkiss
S R & A S Hodgson
S D Holden
Mark J Holt
Stephen Holt

Chris Hooker
Emily Hooper
Gary Horrocks
Chris R Houghton
Barry Howard
Kevan Howarth
Phil Howcroft (Nottingham)
David Hughes
Mr Keith Innes
Derek James
Trevor James
Edna R Jenkins
Richard Jenkins
David Kaye
Andrew Knowles
H Kotowski
R H Kotowski
Z Kotowski
Derek Latham
Michael Latham
Frank Lawrenson
Dr John Leneghan
John Lever
Wayne Lloyd
Caroline Lochhead
N Lofthouse OBE
Derek Longworth
Graham E Lunn
D McBain
John Roy McDonald
I P McDonough
Ian McHugh
Alastair McIlwaine
Colin Magenty
Keith F Makin
Roderick James Mark-Bell
Alistair Marland
Clair Marland
Janet R Marland
Derek G Marsden
Stephen James Marsden
David W Marsh
David & Carol Marshall
Philip Massey
C J Meadows
Steve Mitchell
Andrew Charles Moir
Katy Murphy
Simon E Nightingale
Martin Nisbet
Andrew Norris
Anthony Tom Nuttall
Vernon Nuttall

Frank O'Connell
Chris O'May
Anthony Owen
Carl Owen
Christopher F Parker
Chris Partington
Timothy Mark Partington
Michael E Peachey (and
  family)
Trevor Peacock
John Christopher Pendlebury
Paul Pennington
Barry & Scott Pepper
Sidney Charles Pepper
Frank Phythian
John Pietralski
Phillip Power
Julie Purslow
David Anthony Queen
Annie Ramwell
J Nicholas Rhatigan
Michael Aidan Richards
Eileen F Rigby
Michael Rigby
Shaun Rigby
Thomas Rigby
David J Roberts
Geoff Robinson
Dave Rothwell
Gary Rowson
David Sanger

Peter Scholes
Robert Scholes
Geoff Scott
B Scowcroft
Andrew Sculthorpe
Bob Seddon
G Seymour
David Shallcross
Stanley Shaw
Nigel Sheppard
Neil Alec Simmons
Michael Singleton
Bernard Slater
Richard Slater
P John Smalley
Drew Smith
Jack Wilson Smith
Mr G F Southgate
Peter A Stafford
David Stevens
Mark Stewart
B J Swift
J B Taylor
Robert Lawrence Taylor
Mr Alan Robert Thompson
David E Thompson
Mark J Topham
Darren John True
Stephen Wayne True
M Turner
Norman Vickers

Julie Walker
William Farnworth Walker
Mr Alan Walmsley
Mr Lee Walmsley
John Walsh OBE
Peter G Walton
G Warburton
W B Warburton
Joanne Ward
Michael Warren
Ian Watson
Ernest Weall
Norman Weall
Mr Stephen Weir
Mr K A Whitehead
D W Wilde
Graham Wilkinson
Hannah Rose Williams
Danny Wilson
David Ian Wilson
Ian Wilson
Mark J Wilson
Dave 'Wuff' Wolfendale
David W Wolstencroft
Melvyn & Neil Woodcock
Eric Woolfenden
Bruce Wright
John Wroe
Michael & Jennifer Yates